FIVE FAMOUS OPERAS
AND THEIR BACKGROUNDS

Five Famous Operas
and
Their Backgrounds

HELEN L. KAUFMANN

and

HENRY SIMON

Garden City, New York

DOUBLEDAY & COMPANY, INC.

1973

ISBN: 0-385-06147-1 Trade
0-385-01869-x Prebound
Library of Congress Catalog Card Number 72–92395

Contents

INTRODUCTION

My friend Henry Simon conceived the idea of this book, and it is everyone's misfortune that he died when he had finished writing but one opera, *Carmen*, leaving one up and four to go. He enjoyed what he described as a lifelong love affair with grand opera, and paid special tribute to his love in *A Festival of Opera*, a book to which I have gratefully referred in my research on *Don Giovanni, Aïda, Fidelio,* and *Boris Godunov*. Solid scholarship as well as affection gave what he wrote a special quality.

I was honored when Rosalind Simon asked me to complete the volume of *Five Famous Operas* that her husband had started. In the many books I have written about music and musicians, only one, *The Story of 100 Operas*, deals specifically with grand opera. Yet in all humility I agreed to carry on where Henry left off, and I hope that I have done justice to his concept.

There have been murmurs of late that grand opera as we know it is a thing of the past, that new, live, "relevant" stories and styles expressive of the turmoil of the current decade must replace the old. Perhaps supplement is a better word than replace. Certain operas, inspired and imperishable, rise like mountain peaks and continue to dominate the operascape. The fame of the five that have been selected is undisputed and indisputable. They have stood the test of time, have held their place in history and in the hearts of their public. They represent the best of opera by the best of composers of different periods, nationalities, and viewpoints—Mozart, Beethoven, Verdi, Mussorgsky, Bizet. One attribute that all these composers have in common is genius.

HELEN L. KAUFMANN

New York, 1973

TO THE READER

If you are about to attend a performance of any one of the operatic masterpieces herein discussed, it will add to your pleasure to do a bit of homework, and acquire at least a bowing acquaintance with it beforehand. If you have already seen and heard a performance in the flesh and long to know more about its composer, plot, and music, this book stands ready to gratify the longing. One more if. If there is no immediate prospect of your attending a public performance, you can do worse than sit beside your record-player, book in hand, as you follow the action and the music on one of the excellent recordings available. In the past, it was the sport of royalty to attend command performances of operas. Thanks to the introduction of the printed word in the 1400s, and the invention of the record-player in the 1900s, a command performance is now within the reach of everyone. Congratulations to those who seize the opportunity to revel in this way in *Carmen, Don Giovanni, Aïda, Fidelio,* and *Boris Godunov,* each an immortal masterpiece.

Mozart's
DON GIOVANNI

MOZART'S

Don Giovanni

A young man named Don Giovanni
Had for ladies charisma uncanny.
At his call and his beck
They were ready to neck,
Wherever the nook or the cranny.
The fair Donna Anna he had
But he reckoned without her old dad.
Papa did pursue,
The Don ran him through.
Alas! Donna Anna was mad.

Here, in frivolous terms, is the core of the tragicomedy of *Don Giovanni,* the tiny acorn from which grew the mighty oak of Mozart's finest opera, pronounced by such authorities as Rossini, Gounod, and Wagner the greatest of all operas by all composers. How could anyone, even Wolfgang Amadeus Mozart, compose sublime music on such a trite theme? But he was Mozart. He could and did effect the happy marriage between text and music, which constitutes opera at its best, with no thought of divorce or even temporary separation.

The handsome hero of *Don Giovanni* loves girls and leaves them. Like a butterfly, he flits from blossom to blossom, from each extracting its nectar, leaving it to wilt, perhaps to die. What

makes him behave this way? Is it pure, or impure wickedness?
According to the legend of the original Spanish Don Juan, that
gentleman was an idealist, searching for the impossible "she"
whom he could truly love, from whom he would never be able
to part, the compound of flesh and spirit that would blend
eternally with his own. To find her, he tested numerous ladies,
seeking, always seeking.

This is at least one way to explain the length of the catalogue
of lorn ladies recited by the Don's servant, Leporello, as he
unrolls a scroll listing his master's amorous exploits. This he
does with relish for the benefit of a persistent and unwanted
admirer. Mozart and his librettist, Lorenzo da Ponte, must have
chuckled like a couple of school boys as they elaborated this
and other incidents, da Ponte to make the most of them in
words and action, Mozart in enduring music. The plot they
finally evolved consisted of two close-packed acts, with five
scenes each, a full evening's complement of kaleidoscopic action.

THE CAST

Don Giovanni, hero and villain	Baritone or bass
Don Pedro, the "Commendatore" (Commandant),	
father of Donna Anna	Bass
Don Ottavio, fiancé of Donna Anna	Tenor
Leporello, more villain than angel,	
servant of Don Giovanni	Bass
Masetto, a peasant with a mind of his own	Bass or Baritone
Zerlina, Masetto's flirtatious fiancée	Soprano
Donna Anna, the hero's Nemesis	Soprano
Donna Elvira, faithful though betrayed	Soprano

*There is a chorus of peasants, musicians, dancers, etc., who appear
at appropriate moments. The action takes place in Seville. The time
is the middle of the seventeenth century.*

THE STORY

ACT I

The curtain rises on a garden in Seville. It is night. Leporello is there, waiting for his master to come from the house, and
feeling sorry for himself because he has to work so hard finding
new ladies for Don Giovanni, who has all the fun, while he has
none. Don Giovanni, meanwhile, has tricked his way into the
house, where dwells the carefully guarded Donna Anna, daughter of the "Commendatore," the Commander of Seville. Under
cover of the darkness he has convinced the servant that he is
Don Ottavio, Donna Anna's fiancé, and has been readily ad-
mitted. It is not long, however, before Donna Anna comes
rushing into the garden, clinging to the disguised Don Giovanni.
"You shall not escape," she screams, words seemingly prompted
by fear, but in reality by satisfaction with so ardent a lover.
Enter her irate father, roused from slumber by her cries. He
challenges the unknown intruder to a duel on the spot. He is an
old man, and no match for the Don, who would much prefer
to forget the whole thing. But the Commander stubbornly insists. Don Giovanni, an expert swordsman, disarms him with a
flick of the wrist and, as the Commendatore stumbles forward,
accidentally kills him. He and Leporello run away as Donna
Anna returns with Don Ottavio and servants. She swoons over
her father's body. The alarm is sounded; servants, police, townsfolk come running. There is nothing left for the bereft daughter
but to swear undying vengeance. Furthermore, she makes Don
Ottavio swear with her, and together they vow they will not

marry until the murderer is found and punished, though it takes the rest of their lives.

The scene changes. On a road leading from Seville, the Don and Leporello, still escaping, come upon a beautiful lady in distress. Always on the alert for fresh adventure, the Don approaches her with intent to console in his own fashion. She sobs out her story, and only then does he recognize her as Donna Elvira. He has good reason to shun her. He has enticed her from a convent with the promise of marriage but tired of her and deserted her after three days of connubial bliss. Naturally, she is furious at him; unnaturally, she still loves him, and longs to win him back. He takes French leave, allowing his servant to remain behind and make the necessary explanations. Even when Leporello cynically recites the list of her sisters in misery—2,065 or so—she insists that she is the only one, that she will follow her beloved to the ends of the earth. This is an evidence of constancy to end all constancy, especially in view of the convincing aria sung by Leporello, to these words, translated from the Italian:

> Milady, here is the catalog
> Of the beauties that my lord has loved.
> I have made a list of every one;
> Come and scan it, read it with me.
>
> In Italy six hundred and forty,
> In Germany two hundred thirty-one,
> A hundred in France, in Turkey ninety-one,
> While in Spain already a thousand and three!
>
> Now, among them there were countesses,
> Servant girls and citizens,
> Princesses and marchionesses,

There were ladies of every station,
Every form and every age.

With the blondes it is his custom
To commend their gentle manners,
With the brunettes, constancy,
With the fair ones, their sweet ways.
He wants the plump ones in December,
But in June, they must be slender,
While the tall ones must be stately
And the small ones must be sprightly.
Old ones too he has not missed,
Just to have them on his list;
But his favorite form of sinning
Is with one who's just beginning.
Whether they be rich or poor,
Fair or ugly, one thing's sure;
Just provided they are women,
You know well what happens then;

Now from Italy and Germany,
A hundred odd I've listed here
And then I don't know how many
From France and from Iberia:
There were ladies, there were citizens,
There were countesses and artisans
Servants, cooks and scullery maids,
Needing only to be women
For him to love them, every one.

Such a lover, I must tell you,
Were he to keep all his promises,
Some day he'd find himself becoming
Husband to the whole wide world.
I must tell you, he'll have any,
Be they plump or be they skinny,

> Since 'tis none except the old ones
> Fail to set his heart aflame.
> You know how he is!

Despite the catalogue, Donna Elvira insists that she is the one and only, that it is she and she alone whom he loves. She will search for him to the ends of the earth, and win him back, come what may.

When next seen, the Don is outside his own palace, making passes at a pretty peasant girl, Zerlina. She and her sweetheart, Masetto, have been dancing with friends to celebrate their approaching wedding. The Don joins the dance, his right as lord of the manor. He selects Zerlina as his partner, and in no time bewitches her with flattery and glittering promises. He commands Leporello to invite the whole party into the castle, leaving him alone with Zerlina. By now, Masetto is suspicious, but dares not disobey, and unwillingly joins the others. In a most seductive duet, Don Giovanni invites Zerlina to give him her hand (Duet: Give me your hand, beloved). He has almost succeeded in enticing her into the shrubbery, when Donna Elvira interrupts. She makes a dramatic entrance, warning, "Beware!" She scolds the Don roundly. He tries to persuade Zerlina that Elvira's mind is unhinged because she loves him. Nevertheless Elvira succeeds in dragging his intended victim away from him. By the happy coincidence peculiar to opera plots, Donna Anna and Don Ottavio happen to pass by. They greet Don Giovanni as friends, and when Donna Elvira tells them her story, they believe that she is mad. But Donna Anna is uneasy. There is something in the Don's voice which recalls that of her would-be seducer. Never having seen him in daylight, she doesn't know what he looks like, nor who he is; his voice is her only clue. She and Don Ottavio go off, leaving the Don with Donna Elvira, whom Leporello presently takes off his hands.

A pretty scene outside the villa follows. Masetto comes in search of Zerlina, they kiss and make up, she promises to be a good girl and flirt no more. "Beat me, beat me, dear Masetto, if I do," she begs. But the Don returns, having got rid of Donna Elvira, and firmly leads the young couple into the villa, where their friends are drinking and making merry. Three masked strangers knock at the gate and are invited to come in and crash the party. They are, of course, Donna Elvira, Donna Anna, and Don Ottavio, who have joined forces against Don Giovanni.

When the merriment is at its height, Don Giovanni invites Zerlina to be his partner in the Minuet. Thrilled, yet frightened, she gives him her hand, while Leporello, under orders, maneuvers Masetto to the opposite end of the ballroom. In the mazes of the dance, the Don adroitly leads his intended prey into an adjoining chamber. A piercing shriek sounds above the gentle strains of the Minuet. Masetto breaks away from Leporello and rushes to the rescue of his beloved. The Don is pursued from bedroom to ballroom by the enraged bridegroom and his bride. The three masked guests join the peasants in a chorus of outrage. Don Giovanni cries that Leporello is to blame. Brandishing his sword, he flees for his life, driving Leporello before him. The act ends in a scene of stormy confusion, underlined by the rumble of thunder from the brasses in the orchestra, flashes of lightning from the strings, and a chorus of anger from the guests.

ACT II

When the Second Act opens, the Don has recovered his composure. He and Leporello are standing in the street beneath Donna Elvira's balcony. Leporello announces that he is quitting, but the Don only laughs, and tosses him a purse. "All right," says Leporello, "if you'll stop womanizing I'll stay." The Don exclaims, "Certainly not! Women are more necessary to me than the bread I eat, the air I breathe." And as he hears Donna Elvira lamenting from her balcony the loss of his affections, he concocts a new, cruel stratagem to add to her suffering. He proceeds to outline it to Leporello. The servant is to impersonate him, he, the servant. They change clothes on the spot. He hides under Elvira's balcony, urging her to come down to him. Enraptured by his voice, she agrees. Leaving Leporello to continue the masquerade with her, the Don, disguised as Leporello, sings the loveliest of serenades to her maid. All very well, but things don't work out as expected. Masetto and friends appear on the scene, armed with clubs, determined to give the Don a good drubbing. Finding Leporello disguised, they believe he is the Don at his old tricks, making love to Donna Elvira. They set to with right good will, and lambaste him thoroughly. Leporello's outcries reach the Don's ears, and he comes to the rescue of his supposed master. Leporello takes himself off, while the Don, in his servant's clothes, sends the peasants in different directions in search of himself. But he holds on to Masetto and, when the others have left, beats him unmercifully, leaving him groaning on the ground before making his own triumphant getaway. Here Zerlina, seeking her Masetto with a lantern, finds him. She comforts him with loving caresses and renewed vows to be faithful forever and ever, amen. But the episode is not yet ended. In Donna Elvira's garden, Leporello, still in the Don's clothes, is attacked by Donna Anna, the disillusioned Donna Elvira, and Zerlina, with Masetto and Ottavio to enforce their demands with clubs. He has a bad time warding off their blows while he convinces them that he is not the person his clothes indicate. Finally, badly battered, he is permitted to escape.

He is next seen in a churchyard, where he meets Don Giovanni. Each man is now dressed as himself. It is 2 A.M. The graveyard is spooky and Leporello is scared. But the Don, in spite of the somber surroundings, greets him jovially, behaves as though nothing has occurred, and bursts into a description of his latest conquest. Here, the supernatural enters the picture. The statue guarding the grave of Donna Anna's father, the Commendatore, comes to life and in a sepulchral bass voice orders Don Giovanni to desist from his blasphemy and to change his ways, or else—! Leporello, shaking with fright, tries to run away, but the Don, undaunted, stands firm. With a defiant laugh, he commands his trembling servant to invite the Commendatore to dinner the next evening. When Leporello refuses, he himself issues the invitation, and the statue grimly nods acceptance.

In the final scene, Don Giovanni, in his palace, awaits the arrival of his guest. He dresses in his best, orders his private orchestra to entertain him, and seats himself at the dining table. He commands Leporello to serve the meal and pour the wine. While they feast merrily, Donna Elvira comes to make a last desperate appeal that her lover reform, save his soul, and live happily with her forever after. The two men deride and mock her. Finally, affronted, she opens the door to leave them but turns back with a loud cry and sinks fainting to the floor. Heavy footsteps are heard, then a sharp knock at the door. Leporello hides under the table. The Don, sword in hand, flings open the door. With heavy tread, the stone statue steps in. Grasping the Don's hand, he invites him for the last time to repent. With haughty defiance, Don Giovanni refuses. A flash of lightning, a thunderclap, the floor gapes open, and the Don disappears into the infernal regions.

The opera actually should end here. Mozart himself, in the version he offered in Vienna in 1788, did stop at this point. But at the first performance in Prague, in 1787, lest vice appear more attractive than virtue, he tacked on a sextet by Donna Anna, Donna Elvira and Company, warning the wicked against the consequences of wrongdoing. It is difficult not to smile at this contrived moralistic ending, after the general gaiety, where even the hero's hypocrisy and cruelty are lightly treated. We can imagine composer and librettist having a good laugh over the finale as they tossed off a convivial glass of wine in the coffeehouse, where they met to mull over what they had done. As a matter of fact, the sextet is an imposing piece, a great addition to the score. Neither man was actually responsible for the plot. The story of the original Don Juan appeared in many forms and with various endings before da Ponte was inspired to clothe it anew in Italian verse.

In the early 1600s, there was a Spanish play, *El Burlador de Sevilla* (The Libertine of Seville), by a certain Tirso de Molina (1571–1641), a presumably true or partly true account of the amours of a wealthy Spanish nobleman, Don Juan Tenorio. The story, infectiously entertaining, wandered as widely afield as did its hero. From Spain to Germany to Italy it traveled, its outline the same, its details freely varied. In 1665, Molière, the foremost French playwright of his day, produced *Le Festin de Pierre* (The Stone Banquet). He not only transformed the Spanish nobleman into an equally dissolute French aristocrat, but introduced a new victim, Elvira, whom the Don persuades to leave her convent, only to desert her after three days of mock marriage. Molière's play has no Donna Anna and Don Ottavio, but instead creates Masetto and Zerlina, the young couple who do much to heighten and brighten the music and action in Mozart's opera. In seventeenth-century England, *The Libertine,* a play with incidental music by the famous English composer Henry Purcell, inducted the staid British public into the facts of life (that is, vicious life) via Don Juan. In 1739 a young Italian, Carlo Goldoni, wrote *Don Giovanni Tenorio ossia Il Dissoluto* (Don Giovanni Tenorio, or The Rake). Goldoni apologized in advance for selecting so indecent a subject. He wrote, "I have always regarded it in Italy with horror, and I have never been able to understand how this farce could hold its own for such a long time, could draw crowds, and could be the delight of a cultivated nation." Yet, in view of the fact that Molière had found it a not unworthy story, Goldoni tackled it, "in order to fulfill the contract with the devil a bit more fittingly." Ironically, because of his attempt to compromise with the devil, his play is less effective than those which dramatize and glorify the hero's iniquities, as da Ponte's version did.

Da Ponte was perhaps most strongly influenced by a more recent work, an opera performed in Venice in 1787, with words by Giovanni Bertati, music by Giuseppe Gazzaniga. He may have suggested the subject to Mozart with the shrewd idea of making his own task easier by borrowing from it. His version shows traces of Bertati, Molière, and Gluck, as well as Goldoni, but in the end his text surpassed them all, his flowing Italian lines a perfect complement to Mozart's music.

Twenty-three operas about Don Juan have been written, a fair indication of the fascination the subject holds for audiences. Though worked over and over, the story has not become trite or dated but retains its hold on the imagination.

No doubt Mozart envisaged himself as Don Juan, the irresistible, insatiable lover, while da Ponte saw himself as Leporello, "a mixture of wit, impertinence, cowardice, gluttony,

and a hundred other characteristics of the typical servant, one of
the oldest stock characters in history." Both reveled in their
fantasy. In 1787, when Mozart composed the music, four years
before his untimely death at thirty-five, he still showed the
after-effects of his underprivileged and deprived youth. Underprivileged? Mozart, the wonder-child, the darling of princely
salons, the recipient of kisses from an empress and favors from
kings, the peripatetic little genius who had only to shake his
sleeve to produce from its lacy folds a sheaf of eternal music!
Mozart underprivileged? Yes, truly, Mozart.

Let us look objectively at the picture of his youth, noting
particularly the powerful paternal thumb under which he spent
it. As soon as his genius was recognized, at the tender age of
four, he was compelled to become its slave. From then on, his
leisure moments were few and far between. Leopold Mozart,
a strict pedagogue in anybody's terms, made sure that his poten-
tially profitable son spent his waking hours studying, practicing,
or composing. The child wrote until his fingers were so stiff
that he could no longer hold the pen. Child labor, eighteenth-century model. Wolfgang obeyed rules more numerous and
binding than the Ten Commandments given to Moses on Mount
Sinai. Such were his irrepressible high spirits and the love of
life inherited from his mother, that outwardly he throve under
the treatment. But even while he was growing to manhood, the
restrictions were barely relaxed. To be sure, he went to parties
where he danced with the girls, who flirted and flattered, but he
was always under observation. Two possessive parents and one
equally possessive sister joined forces to keep such relationships
from going beyond the utmost innocence. Until he was twenty-
one, Wolfgang never traveled without his father. He ate, slept,
worked, played as ordained. Even when he had come of age and
dared to rebel against Archbishop Colloredo, his hated employer,

he remained enslaved. Both he and his father played in the archbishop's orchestra in Salzburg; it was their bread and butter. Wolfgang resigned from the orchestra and left Salzburg to seek his fortune. But even then he was not free. His mother went along, since his father dared not leave the job. She was given strict injunctions to report everything in minute detail and, above all, to keep her charge out of mischief, mischief being Leopold Mozart's synonym for love.

On that trip the inevitable happened. Mozart did fall in love. The object of his affections was Aloysia Weber, the sixteen-year-old daughter of a copyist connected with the Mannheim Opera. The Webers had four girls, and the attentions of a marriageable young man were welcome. Aloysia was vastly more sophisticated than Wolfgang and she flattered him. She sang his songs and sang them beautifully, hoping that he would be successful and help her to build her own career. She was coldly calculating, he was madly in love, his first love. His mother, alarmed, dutifully wrote all the details to her husband. Equally dutifully, she lost no time in obeying the peremptory order that came by slow coach from Salzburg, to move on. They had been six months waiting for the appointment from the Elector of Mannheim that never came. Fortified by authority, she carried off her son to Paris, away from temptation. (A strange description of Paris!) While he moped and mooned, Aloysia, who had promised to marry him, gave what heart she had to a more solvent suitor. As if this were not enough of a blow, his mother fell ill and died suddenly in Paris, far from home. He was desolate and alone. For the first time in his life there was no one to tell him what to do. He was free, as he had longed to be, but now that he had his freedom, he had no idea what to do with it. As a tame bird, released, has been known to do, he flew back into the Salzburg cage, though not without a protesting chirp. He had to borrow money to return. He stopped en route in Munich, still hoping for an appointment there, but disappointment awaited. Aloysia made it unmistakably clear that she had no intention of marrying him. He was brokenhearted. For consolation, he stopped in Augsburg to visit his cousin Maria Anna Mozart, nicknamed "Bäsle." Since he had been a small boy, he had corresponded with her in bantering, lover-like fashion. Now they talked of marriage, but his father and sister Nannerl quashed that project quickly by their hostility when Bäsle came for an exploratory visit.

Mozart was small, delicate, not handsome, not a good financial prospect. Women did not swoon at his approach nor vie for his favors. Two possible romances with Salzburg maidens came to nothing. What was a normal young man to do with all the amorous passion pent up within him? When Mozart finally married Aloysia Weber's younger sister Constanze, inveigled by her mother into taking that bold step against the opposition of his family, his desire knew no bounds. Too long controlled, it burst forth like a tidal wave engulfing him completely. For six of the nine years of their marriage, Constanze was pregnant. When they were separated, his letters to his "dear little wife" make no secret of the way in which he missed her most. Like Oliver Twist, he wanted more. His appetite, once aroused, was insatiable.

Probably no woman could have completely satisfied him; Constanze certainly could not. She had not the education, the breeding, the understanding to be a mate for a Mozart. She was a child bride, and remained so, frivolous, extravagant, and spoiled, though loving and responsive to his passion.

He dreamed of being the Great Lover, rich, handsome, irresistible. He tried to be true to Constanze after his fashion, but what was that fashion? At the very moment of his success, when Constanze was with him in Prague for the rehearsals of *Don Giovanni*, there were rumors that he was dallying with the women in the cast—Donna Anna (Teresa Saporiti), Donna Elvira (Caterina Mirelli), and Zerlina (Caterina Bondini), all three at the same time. Especially imprudent was this, for Mme. Bondini was the wife of the impresario who had commissioned the opera. But how indicative it was of the probability that Mozart, carried away by the character of Don Giovanni, was acting with all the reckless disregard of consequences of the Don himself. As a little boy, he had asked everyone engagingly, "Do you love me?" As a man, he continued to ask and to hope. Like the Don, he was searching for the mate who would assuage his craving for more than physical gratification, a craving that Constanze was unfit to comprehend, far less to appease.

If Mozart was Don Giovanni, da Ponte was Leporello. Immensely tall, he towered over the small, slender composer like de Gaulle over Napoleon. A flowing cape, a swarthy skin, and glittering black eyes gave him the appearance of a gypsy conjuror. A conjuror of sorts he was, a romantic adventurer. He juggled books and accounts, people, and often-dubious activities with the skill of a professional magician. An ordained priest and a teacher, he landed in Vienna, coming from Venice and Dresden, seeking his fortune, but suffering much misfortune due to his profligate ways. Often he escaped an irate husband or pursuing creditor by the skin of his teeth. His motto seems to have been "Lead me into temptation, and see what I can do."

In Vienna, the temptation took the form not only of light love but of light opera. He proved the perfect librettist for Mozart's opera *The Marriage of Figaro*, which preceded *Don Giovanni* and is, in fact, largely responsible for the existence of that masterpiece. The Emperor of Austria, Joseph II, had a secret yen for Italian opera, which he decided to indulge when a German opera company he had engaged failed to please him. He commissioned several new works in his favorite tongue; da Ponte was to supply the text for an opera by Salieri, one by Martin Soler, one by Mozart. Da Ponte and Mozart agreed on the story of *The Marriage of Figaro* for good reasons. Paisiello's opera *The Barber of Seville* had created the character of the busy barber Figaro, based on a play by the French playwright Beaumarchais, in which they saw infinite possibilities. Beaumarchais had carried his story a step further in a sequel, *Le Mariage de Figaro*. It contained satirical comments on the naughty haughty aristocrats who constituted the "Establishment" of the eighteenth century, and the play could not be performed in Vienna because it was "subversive." But it could still be bought in the bookstores, and both men read it. They agreed that since the music would cover up all objectionable remarks, they were not taking a chance in making it into an opera. They followed the principle enunciated by Figaro: "Ce qui ne vaut pas la peine d'être dit, on le chante." (What one daren't say, one sings.)

Following Beaumarchais' play rather closely, da Ponte set the text in the Italian he and the Emperor preferred to all other tongues. Mozart clothed it in bright, meaningful melody. It took him only six weeks to complete the score. The friends who dropped in to listen and comment while sipping Constanze's punch and coffee were so enthusiastic that the two men fondly hoped that they had tapped a goldmine, that appointments for a term as court composer and court librettist would inevitably follow. They were blind to the hard fact of the Emperor's thrift. He was paying a retainer of two thousand gulden per annum as court composer to Christoph Willibald Gluck, an established German who had been partly Italianized. Salieri was also on the payroll. Emperor Joseph was too economical to add another regular salary to his budget, however talented the recipient.

He did, however, make one concession, urged by that persuasive publicity man da Ponte. He took an afternoon off to listen while Mozart played and sang what he had done, an audition with piano. Completely captivated, the Emperor ordered his chamberlain, Count Rosenberg, to make arrangements at once to have the opera produced, all expenses paid. The Count also was captivated, but he reacted differently. He engaged the best singers and players, as instructed, but, green with jealousy, he schemed at the same time against the success of *The Marriage of Figaro*. The Emperor attended the dress rehearsal, where all went marvelously well.

At the opening performance, May 1, 1786, Joseph was in the royal box, surrounded by his court, Count Rosenberg beside him, the house overflowing. When Mozart took his place at the clavier from which he conducted, the applause was deafening. An expectant silence fell. Count Rosenberg smiled evilly and waited. Mozart gave the orchestra the signal for the overture. Horrors! What was this? A wrong chord, then another, a muddle of sounds. He could not believe his ears. The carefully rehearsed, merry overture was a catastrophe. The strings played out of tune, they made wrong entrances. The singers too joined in the sabotage. They missed their cues, sang *forte* when *piano* was indicated, and vice versa. Their acting was deplorable, awkward, and stumbling. Mozart frantically beat time, sang their parts, pounded the clavier, implored them sotto voce to behave. But they didn't.

At the end of the first act, Mozart hurried to the imperial box. "Your Majesty," he whispered, his lips so dry he could barely form the words. Of course Joseph had realized at once

that something was wrong. Hadn't he heard the dress rehearsal? Didn't he know the music? He frowned at Count Rosenberg, who stood with ears cocked, awaiting the hisses he had
paid for, as he had paid for the misbehavior on stage. "Go and
tell those singers to stop their treachery instantly and sing that
opera as they should; otherwise they shall leave my service instantly, and there will be no more opera in Vienna," he snapped.
There was nothing for the Count to do but to execute the
royal command. The next three acts went swimmingly. Every
aria was encored until the Emperor called a halt to the applause, and even so the performance lasted until early morning.
Then Mozart, da Ponte, and Constanze, tired but happy,
tumbled into a carriage and rode home in triumph, singing
Figaro's hit song, *non più andrai*, at the top of their lungs.

Whether or not this melodramatic account of the underhand
doings of Mozart's enemies is wholly true, it does underline the
difficulties that he had to contend with. He had jealous com-
petitors who conspired against him. *The Marriage of Figaro*,
generally and genuinely popular as it was, was performed in
Vienna nine times in eight months and then dropped. Nor were
the collaborators out of the financial woods, for they were paid
a lump sum which was soon spent, and after that, nothing.
Whether the houses were full or empty, they had nothing to
gain. Mozart seriously considered trying his luck in England,
where he had friends and a reputation. He went so far as to
write to his father, asking him to baby-sit with the two children
in Salzburg while he and Constanze were away. Leopold in-
dignantly refused to be saddled with such a responsibility, and
the trip to England had to be abandoned.

As it happened, this turned out to be all for the best. In
early April 1787, Wolfgang and Constanze were invited to
Prague, the capital of music-loving Bohemia, today Czecho-

slovakia. *The Marriage of Figaro* had been performed there and had been pronounced the hit of the opera season. Mozart wrote from Prague to a friend in Vienna, "Here they talk of nothing but *Figaro,* visit no opera but *Figaro,* and eternally *Figaro.*" At balls and parties everyone danced to tunes from *Figaro,* and even in the lowliest coffeehouses they were played, sung, and whistled. He basked in the success of *Figaro,* and in the warm welcome of the townspeople. Also, he enjoyed the special friendship of two illustrious couples. Count Johann Joseph Thun provided bed and board and luxurious living quarters in his palace. Franz and Josepha Duschek, whom Mozart had known in Salzburg, lived close to the Thun palace, and the Mozarts had the run of their lovely house and garden. Musicians thronged the Duscheks' morning, noon, and night. More important still, partly through their influence, partly because of the success of *The Marriage of Figaro,* Mozart was offered one hundred ducats by the new impresario of the Prague opera, Pasquale Bondini, to write an opera. It had to be done quickly, for it was to be produced the following autumn for a special occasion. There was no time to be lost. Bondini was gambling that Mozart could do it, that the new opera would be as great or a greater success than *The Marriage of Figaro,* and that he, Bondini, would reap some of the credit.

Naturally Mozart went at once to da Ponte, and da Ponte suggested Don Juan as the subject. It appealed so strongly to both of them that they plunged in without delay. Had it not been for the triumph of *The Marriage of Figaro,* da Ponte might have missed out on this, his grand opportunity for lasting fame; Mozart's greatest opera might never have been born. For this reason, it has seemed fitting to dwell at some length on *The Marriage of Figaro,* since their collaboration here sparked *Don Giovanni,* a unique masterpiece. They were destined to do but one more opera together after *Don Giovanni—Così fan tutte.*

Much of the score and libretto of *Don Giovanni* were composed in Vienna, after the January visit to Prague. Mozart had other obligations also to fulfill in Vienna during the summer. But in July he fell desperately ill with a fever, and lay in the hospital for a month, visited daily by his alarmed doctor. He was deeply depressed. Constanze was ailing at home. He had lost a close friend, Count Hatzfeld, his father had died in May, and the sense of loss was keen. But for him there was no better cure than a contract for an opera. While he lay in bed, he spun melodies and as he regained his strength, he stored them in his mind. When he had returned from the hospital, Constanze, lying in bed in the morning, heard him humming and knocking his heels together as he splashed the water about, a sure sign that he was at work in his own way. "I am writing this opera for Bondini, surely, and for the people of Prague, too—but mostly for myself and my friends," he confided in one of his letters.

Da Ponte, meanwhile, was writing the text not only of *Don Giovanni,* but of two other operas. When he went to the Emperor to report to him that he was doing so, Joseph laughed. "You can't," he said. "Perhaps not," replied da Ponte, "but I intend to try. At night I shall write for Mozart; in the morning for Martin; in the evening for Salieri." The Emperor shook his head, which made da Ponte all the more determined. He set to work immediately, placing a decanter of wine at his right, a box of snuff at his left, and an inkstand right in the middle of his desk. Oh yes, one thing more. He arranged with his landlady that her daughter, a pretty sixteen-year-old should remain close at hand. While he scribbled for hours, she sat in an adjoining room with a book or embroidery, and came to him at the first tinkle of the bell on his desk. He wrote roguishly in his

Memoirs that she brought him now a little cake, now a cup of coffee, now "anything he asked for." Her gay, smiling face and willing care inspired him to write Zerlina's lines with wit and tenderness.

At the end of August, the Mozarts left for Prague. Wolfgang was fully recovered, Constanze was uncomfortably pregnant. They both looked forward to the spicy Prague ham, the beer, the friends, the gay conviviality of their previous visit. As the coach wended its slow way, Mozart sat back against the cushions, drumming his fingers, crossing and uncrossing his legs, making faces. Once in a while, he nodded with satisfaction, and jotted down a few notes on a scrap of paper he took from his pocket. Constanze, in her corner, watched him but didn't speak. Often, while composing, he begged her to talk to him, tell him stories, keep one half of him entertained while the other half worked. In the coach she had enough to do to brace herself against the jolting and bumping over the rutted road, and was well pleased to be silent. When they arrived in Prague, all was hustle and bustle and warm welcome. Bondini had engaged pleasant rooms for them at the Three Golden Lions, a comfortable inn not far from the opera house. He met the coach and saw the visitors well bestowed.

A few days later, da Ponte arrived from Vienna, and was quartered in a room with a balcony, across the street. So scant was the space between their lodgings that the two men could almost shake hands from window to balcony. They shouted jokes or quips or bits of melody or new twists of plot across at each other, much to the amusement of the passers-by in the street beneath their windows, and finished many an argument over a mug of beer or a glass of wine in the neighboring coffeehouse. Here they were sometimes joined by Casanova, the famous lover whose exploits equaled Don Juan's. His memories of a ribald past, later embodied in his autobiography, he shared with them and further enlivened the plot of the opera.

This ideal arrangement was terminated when da Ponte had been in Prague barely a week. A peremptory message summoned him to Vienna, to deliver the text of Salieri's opera, *Axur, Re d'Ormus*. He dared not refuse, though it meant that he would be obliged to miss the first performance of *Don Giovanni* in Prague. What a disappointment! He may even have sensed that he was foregoing an immortal work for the sake of a mediocre though popular one. Surely he cursed his hard luck with picturesque Italian profanity.

When he had gone, the Mozarts moved from the inn to a guest room in the home of their friends, the Duscheks. Here Wolfgang was in heaven. It was warm, and he could work out of doors. While he scribbled away at a table on the terrace, a string quartet practiced in one room of the house, a harpsichordist in another, a singer in another. Music filled the air. Franz Duschek was a pianist, his wife Josepha a soprano; their doors were hospitably open to anyone who loved or practiced music. Bondini the impresario, Strobach the conductor, the young Count Thun and others bowled, and Mozart joined them in a game when he felt the need to get up and stretch. Even so, he never lost the thread of the music he was writing, but turned out pages of neat script which never needed a correction, all in the midst of chatter and laughter, games and dancing, and other people's music. Not for him the solitary, soundproof studio. The convivial sounds of laughter and talk were the electricity that sparked his motor. He said, "I take out of the bag of my memory, if I may use that phrase, what has previously been collected in it. For this reason, the committing to paper is done quickly enough, for everything is already finished, and it rarely differs on paper from what it was in my imagination."

As each singer's part was completed, it was dispatched to him posthaste, to be memorized before rehearsals started. Early in the game, Mozart discovered that the singers in the Prague opera company were "slow studies." They did not memorize easily, and were too lazy and pleasure-loving to make any great effort to meet their assignment on time. They never did today what they could put off until tomorrow. He invited them to join him in the Duschek garden, where he could teach them, parrot fashion if necessary, before turning them loose for the fun and games they preferred. The impresario's budget could not be stretched to include understudies. As it was, *Don Giovanni* was an expensive show to produce. If a principal singer fell ill, the performance was simply canceled or postponed. The premiere of *Don Giovanni* was twice postponed.

The delay was not wholly unwelcome. The first performance, planned for October 14, was to be a gala for a young bride, the Austrian Archduchess Maria Theresa. She intended to stop in Prague on her way to visit Prince Anton of Saxony, to whom she was to be married. Mozart and da Ponte knew this. They knew that the text had to be submitted to the court chamberlain before permission was granted for her to attend. The full text of *Don Giovanni* to an innocent young girl? Mozart and da Ponte ruefully recognized that it would not get past the chamberlain as written. They submitted a specially printed libretto, omitting or softening certain incidents. They reminded each other that, as in *The Marriage of Figaro*, music could convey what words dared not. To make assurance doubly sure, they managed to have the premiere postponed until the Archduchess had left Prague.

In fact, she had gone before the first full stage rehearsal took place on October 22, one week before the opening. Despite Mozart's previous coaching, the mixture did not want to jell at that rehearsal. He missed his well-trained singers of the Vienna Opera, especially as *Don Giovanni* was more difficult for the singers than his previous operas. Signora Bondini, who was cast, or rather miscast, as Zerlina, posed a particular problem. Since she was the wife of the impresario and considered herself Mozart's special friend, she did not take kindly to correction, however badly she sang—and she did sing badly. In the ball-room scene, Mozart's patience gave out. The stage directions called for her to emit a piercing scream as she fled from the bedroom, pursued by Don Giovanni. The feeble squeak she emitted would not have pierced a sheet of tissue paper. After she had made several attempts, Mozart quietly handed the baton to his concertmaster, crept backstage, and, at the cue, stuck a pin into the Signora. Her shriek of pain was as piercing as the pin. "Bravo!" whispered Mozart, as he pushed her onto the stage. "Now go on." She was undecided whether to laugh, cry or stand on her dignity, but she got the idea and gave no further trouble with her *shriek,* at least.

There were daily rehearsals. Every day, Bondini asked Mozart for the overture. Putting the cart before the horse, the composer had written the whole opera, but not the overture which introduced it. "You'll have it, don't worry," was his invariable reply. On the evening before the opening, the Duscheks had a large party. The Mozarts were dancing together when Bondini loomed up beside them. "Where is the overture to *Don Giovanni,* Maestro?" he asked for the umpteenth time. "Here," laughed Mozart, dramatically striking his forehead. Bondini was dismayed, but Mozart poked him in the ribs. "You shall have it in time for the performance," he promised, and calmly continued to dance. Not until he and Constanze had danced to their hearts' content did they leave the party. It was then after midnight. Back in his own room, Mozart became his father's son. He sat down at his writing table and, while Constanze sat beside him and plied him with punch and black coffee, wrote the immortal overture. "Don't go away," he begged her. "Talk to me. Tell me a story, any story, a fairy tale, anything to keep me awake." Like Scheherazade in *The Arabian Nights* she sat with him until the work was done. So compellingly was the overture in his mind that it led, in an impetuous rush, with no break, right into the rise of the curtain on the first act and Leporello's aria in Donna Anna's garden.

On October 29, 1787, the evening of the first performance, all of Prague was agog. A new opera by anyone would have been an event. But one by Wolfgang Amadeus Mozart, composer of *The Marriage of Figaro,* known and loved not only in the palaces, but in the coffeehouses, streets and alleys of Prague was an event with a capital E. Coaches bearing ladies in billowing brocades and sparkling diadems rolled into the square reserved for box holders. Their escorts, in satin breeches and laces, with jeweled scabbards at hip, rode on horseback beside the coaches. The townspeople gathered to gape at royalty as folks do in America at movie stars when a new picture is premiered. The masses thronged into the pit and balcony, the classes took their seats in boxes. There was a hush. The orchestra men were in their places, waiting for Mozart to appear. Five, ten, twenty minutes passed—no Mozart. At last, to the relief of the tense company, the little door under the stage opened. But it was not Mozart who entered. A young man with an armful of music pushed in and quickly distributed the sheets to the players. A few minutes later, to a thunder of applause, Mozart took his place at the clavier. The players did their part so nobly in the overture they read at sight that Mozart whispered to his concertmaster, "A good many notes fell under the desks, but it went off well, just the same."

When the curtain fell at the end of the first act, the roars and cheers, the stamping and the clapping were deafening. But this was as nothing to the applause at the end of the opera. Mozart was hoisted onto the stage to take bow after bow. He was pelted with flowers. Too overcome for speech, he held out his lace-ruffled hands and, with tears running down his cheeks, said simply, "My Prague friends understand me." Success was sweet. He remained in Prague for several more performances.

The Mozarts returned reluctantly to Vienna in November. It was like going from a hothouse of approval to a frigidaire of indifference. Again there was not enough money. Their fourth baby was born, a sickly little girl, and expenses were high. Despite the laurels clinging to his brow, Mozart had to borrow in order to pay the bills. Finally, news of the success in Prague of *Don Giovanni* percolated to the Emperor Joseph, and he ordered that it be performed for him in Vienna. "The opera is divine, finer perhaps than *Figaro*, but it is not the meat for my Viennese," he said. To which Mozart hotly retorted, "We must give them time to chew it." *Don Giovanni* was labeled by Mozart *opera buffa in due atti*—comic opera in two acts. Da Ponte described his libretto as *dramma giocoso*—gay drama. But the importance given in text and music to the roles of Donna Anna, Donna Elvira, and Don Ottavio invites classification as *opera seria*—grand opera. Just what *is* the overriding mood of this tantalizing opera has been debated since its composition. Dr. Alfred Einstein defines it as *"opera buffa* with *seria* and *buffa* roles,"* that is, comic opera with both tragic and comic roles. This all-embracing description should satisfy the lovers of both types of opera.

An appreciative contemporary critic wrote, "How can this music, so full of force, majesty, and grandeur be expected to please the lovers of ordinary opera? . . . The grand and noble qualities of the music in *Don Giovanni* will appeal only to the small minority of the elect. It is not such as to tickle the ears of the crowd and leave the heart unsatisfied." He agreed with the Emperor Joseph. It is true that *Don Giovanni*, though recognized as a masterpiece and included in the repertory of every self-respecting opera company, is not performed as frequently as more comprehensible, less taxing works. The music demands of singers and players all the technical and interpretative skill they can muster. The scenery and production are expensive; this is no one-set, two-actor, "little theater" production. In its blending of the hilariously comic and the tragically serious, in the speed of its action, the quality of its music and the reality of its personages, especially its hero, there is almost hypnotic fascination. To know it is to love it; to know it well is to love it better. Dark, primeval, elemental forces are combined with wit and humor in drama, words and music, especially music.

To do the music justice in words is impossible. Nor are musical illustrations on the printed page a satisfactory substitute for the music. Such excerpts are necessarily brief, a bare hint of the delightful whole. Those who are somewhat familiar with the opera may turn to a reference work such as *Vocal and Opera Themes,* by Harold Barlow and Sam Morgenstern, to verify or refresh their memory of the parts which have already pleased them. For those who come to *Don Giovanni* as novices, eager to plunge, two invaluable aids are available: a good selection of recordings, and a libretto or score or both. The libretto or score may be used in conjunction with recordings of individual parts of the opera, and, even more helpfully, in following the opera as a whole. While doing so, the listener can pinpoint his own choice of memorable moments, and at the

same time linger over those which are generally considered to be
outstanding. A list of recordings, in alphabetical order, follows:

RECORDINGS*

Danco, Dermota, Corena, Siepi, Krips   4-London 1401
Excerpts from above   London 25115
Nilsson, Arroyo, Talvela, Fischer-Dieskau, Böhm, Prague Nat'l.
    Th.   4-Deutsche Grammophon 271 1006
Excerpts from above   Deutsche Grammophon 136282
Schwarzkopf, Sutherland, Wächter, Taddei, Giulini

                                             4-Angel S-3605
Excerpts from above   Angel S-35642
Sutherland, Lorengar, Horne, Bacquier, Krenn, Gramm, Bonynge,
    Eng. Ch. Orch.   4-London 1434
Excerpts from above   London 26215; M311206 (cassette tape)
Watson, Ludwig, Gedda, Ghiaurov, Klemperer, New Phil. Orch.
                                             4-Angel S-3700

Curtis-Verna, Valletti, Taddei, Rudolf   3-Everest/Cetra S-403-3E
Excerpts from above   Everest/Cetra 7403E
Souez, Helletsgrüber, Pataky, Brownlee, Baccaloni, Busch, Glynde-
    bourne   3-Turnabout 4117/9

Even the most casual glance at this list indicates that the
singers represent the cream of the cream of the musical world.
They are hand-picked and this is especially important in *Don
Giovanni,* where the roles are taxing and difficult to realize on a
recording. Each singer must create by his art, without visual or
dramatic aid, such sharply defined characters as the domineering
Donna Anna; the dignified Commendatore, her father; her hen-
pecked but adoring fiancé, Don Ottavio; the flirtatious, com-

* Taken from Schwann-1 Record & Tape Guide, February 1973, and
from Schwann-2 Record & Tape Guide, Spring 1973.

mon-sensible Zerlina; the stodgily jealous Masetto; the confused, infatuated Elvira; the cowardly, vulgar yet comically likable Leporello; and above all, the Don himself, who reverses Shakespeare's "I must be cruel that I may be kind" and behaves with kindness in order to be cruel. To realize these characters and their drama by musical art alone, as we must do on a recording, is a challenge to every singer, every player in the orchestra.

It goes without saying that a libretto while listening is more than first aid, it is essential. Da Ponte's poetic Italian, so superbly fitted to the music, must be known and loved as part of the whole. Translated, his words help to explain the action and to bring the opera to fuller life. Just as, with the explorer in forest and field, landmarks are necessary, so it is for the listener, the explorer in the operatic wilderness. The high spots provide the skeleton which supports the body.

The contrast between aria and recitative in *Don Giovanni* is not, as in many classic operas, a case of transition from glorious aria to recitativo secco, or dry recitative, dry because of the monotonous plunk-plunk of the accompaniment when the narrator recites events. Mozart's accompaniments, even at these often boring moments, carry on, in subdued fashion, the spirit of the opera, and claim attention because they are varied and dramatic. As for the arias, although sometimes based on supply and demand—that is, supplied by the composer at the insistence of a prima donna or tenor—some are truly memorable. A case in point is Don Ottavio's aria, *Dalla sua pace,* inserted because the tenor in Vienna insisted that he be given more of a chance to show what he could do than his counterpart in Prague. It became one of the memorable arias, a challenge to every aspiring tenor.

In the very beginning of the opera, Leporello's aria *Notte e giorno faticar* (Night and day I wear myself out) is interrupted by Donna Anna's shriek, and after a trio in which she expresses wrath, the Don vexation, and Leporello amusement, she is telling Don Ottavio in eloquent recitative all about her father's murder and her vow to seek revenge. In the very beginning, aria and recitative are thus contrasted.

From the wealth of marvelous song to be marked in score or libretto, the following are especially notable:

ACT I

SCENE 2

Elvira: *Ah! chi mi dice mai quel barbaro dov'è* (Ah! who will ever tell me where that rascal is)

Leporello: *Madamina, il catalogo* (Little lady, the catalog)

SCENE 3

Masetto: *Ho capito, signor, sì!* (I've understood, sir, yes indeed!)

Don Giovanni and Zerlina: *Là ci darem la mano!* (Give me your hand, beloved!), followed by *Andiam andiam, mio bene* (Let's go, let's go, my dearest)

Elvira: *Ah! fuggi il traditor!* (Ah! flee the betrayer!)

Anna: *Or sai chi l'onore* (Now you know who robbed me of my honor)

Ottavio: *Dalla sua pace la mia dipende* (My peace depends on hers)

SCENE 4

Don Giovanni: *Fin ch'han dal vino* (Once they have wine)

SCENE 5

Zerlina: *Batti, batti, o bel Masetto* (Beat me, beat me, dear Masetto)
Anna, Elvira, Ottavio: *Protegga, il giusto cielo* (May a just heaven protect us)

SCENE 6

Anna, Elvira, Ottavio, Zerlina, Masetto: *Traditore, traditore, tutto, tutto, già si sa!* (Betrayer, betrayer, all, all is now revealed!)

ACT II

SCENE 1

Don Giovanni: *Eh via, buffone!* (Come, come, you clown!)
Don Giovanni: *Lasciar le donne? Pazzo!* (Let women be? You're crazy. I need them more than the food I eat, the air I breathe.)
Donna Elvira: *Ah! taci, ingiusto core* (Oh! be still, my hungry capricious heart)
Don Giovanni: *Deh! vieni alla finestra* (Pray, come to the window)
Zerlina: *Vedrai, carino, se sei buonino* (You'll see, dear one, if you'll be just a little bit kind)

SCENE 2

Leporello: *Ah, pietà! Signori miei! Ah, pietà, pietà* (Ah, have pity, gentlemen, have pity, pity!)
Ottavio: *Il mio tesoro intanto, andate, andate a consolar* (My treasure while waiting, go, go to console)
Elvira: *Mi tradì quell'alma ingrata* (That ungrateful rascal betrayed me)

SCENE 3

Statue: *Di rider finirai pria dell'aurora.* (You'll stop laughing before the dawn.)

Leporello: *O statua gentilissima del gran Commendatore* (O most respected statue of the great Commander)

SCENE 4

Donna Anna: *Non mi dir, bell'idol mio, che son' io crudel con te.* (Tell me not, my handsome darling, that I am cruel toward you.)

SCENE 5

Don Giovanni: *Già la mensa è preparata* (Dinner now is ready)

Elvira: *L'ultima prova dell'amor mio ancor vogl'io fare con te.* (The final proof of my love I now wish to bring you.)

Statue: *Don Giovanni, a cenar teco m'invitasti* (Don Giovanni, you invited me to dine with you)

Elvira, Zerlina, Ottavio, Masetto, later joined by Anna and Leporello: *Ah dov'è il perfido?* (Ah, where is the perfidious wretch?)

Ottavio: *Or che tutti, o mio tesoro, Vendicatisiam del cielo* (Now that we are all redeemed by Heaven . . . don't keep me waiting any longer)

Finale: *Questo è il fin di chi fa mal* (Such is the fate of the sinner)

Don Giovanni should have made Mozart's fortune, but, like the more popular *Marriage of Figaro,* it left him with almost empty pockets. The Emperor finally deigned to acknowledge his loyalty by bestowing on him the title of *Kammermusiker* (chamber composer). Even this concession was not without its sting. If Gluck had not died that summer, the Emperor would probably have kept Mozart dangling, tantalizing him with occasional words of praise but never giving him an official title. As it was, when Mozart was suggested to take Gluck's place, the clinching argument was not that he had composed deathless music, but that he could be had for less than half Gluck's salary. Gluck received two thousand gulden a year, Mozart only eight hundred. His Imperial Highness humiliated him further by commissioning so few works that Mozart was moved to comment ruefully on receiving his pay check, "Too much for what I do, too little for what I could do."

Beethoven's
FIDELIO

BEETHOVEN'S

Fidelio, oder Die eheliche Liebe

(Fidelio, or Conjugal Love)

"Ha, revenge at last!" cries the villain, raising high his dagger as he approaches his helpless victim. "Dost know who comes to kill thee? 'Tis I, Pizarro!"

Does this sound like a penny dreadful? A ten-cent comic? A melodrama of the 90s? A parody? It is nothing of the sort. It is the climactic scene of Beethoven's glorious opera, *Fidelio*, which reaches its high point when a slender youth steps between villain and victim, whips a pistol from his belt, and cries, "First you must kill me, his wife, Leonore!" Tableau!

In the space age, such scenes are an anachronism. But the human qualities they denote—wifely love, loyalty, endurance, devotion unto death—pertain to all times and all places. No wonder that the story appealed to Beethoven, a lonely, romantic bachelor of thirty-four, yearning for an ideal woman. He believed he had already found his ideal man in Napoleon, whom he worshiped as the embodiment of democracy. He was in fact working on the *Eroica* (Heroic) Symphony which glorified Napoleon at the very time he was introduced to the dead-and-gone eighteenth-century heroine Leonore. He had dedicated the symphony, his third, to his hero. Napoleon had not yet had himself crowned emperor, Beethoven had not yet, in a disillusioned rage, stamped on the dedication and scratched

Napoleon's name from the title page, storming, "Then he too is nothing more than an ordinary human being! Now he too will trample on all the rights of man and indulge only his ambition, exalt himself above all others, become a tyrant!"

Beethoven was in a receptive mood when the subject of an opera was broached to him. He was working on several compositions, as he liked to do. In his spare time he was writing passionate love letters to Josephine von Deym, a beautiful young woman married to a nobleman more than twice her age. Beethoven had given her piano lessons before her unhappy marriage, and continued to do so for love when her husband no longer had money. Their love burst into flame when Count von Deym died, in 1804, while Beethoven was composing *Fidelio*.

Nevertheless, it probably would not have occurred to him to write an opera about Leonore or anyone if it had not been for the indefatigable director of the Theater an der Wien, Emanuel Schikaneder. Schikaneder deserves a page all to himself in the history of music in Vienna. He had nursed many talents in his years as director of the Theater an der Wien, notably Mozart's. It was he who cajoled Mozart into making an opera of his—Schikaneder's—play *The Magic Flute*, who sang Papageno in the original cast, who worked tirelessly for its success. (He died after its three hundredth performance.) Now he turned his attention to Beethoven, a composer known to the public of the theater through concerts of his earlier works. He consulted with Baron von Braun, who was later to buy the theater, and they approached Beethoven, inviting him to try his hand at an opera. At first, Beethoven was cool to the idea. A symphony was "grand" enough for him. Besides, no story that he knew struck him as being worth all that trouble.

Nevertheless when, on a golden September afternoon in 1803, they asked him to come to hear the synopsis of a play by a French writer, Jean Nicolas Bouilly, he accepted. On the bare stage of the theater, Schikaneder and Baron von Braun awaited him. Beethoven seated himself on a straight-backed chair and filled his pipe in silence. His hearing was already troubling him, and he didn't want other people to know about it. Perhaps he worried that no one would commission music from a deaf composer. Under a gruff exterior he hid his fear that he might not be able to follow the reading, and it was a relief when Schikaneder suggested that Beethoven himself read the story aloud. He cleared his throat and read.

"In ancient Spain, there lived a devoted couple, Florestan and his wife Leonore. They abhorred the dishonesty and cruelty of the governor of Seville, Pizarro, whom they regarded as an enemy, as indeed he was. When Florestan threatened to disclose Pizarro's infamy, Pizarro had him arrested and thrown into prison, and circulated the rumor that he had died there. Leonore, grief-stricken, refused to believe the story. Courageously, she embarked on a search for her husband. But since no Spanish lady of the 1700s roamed the streets without a man to protect her, or at least a duenna, she put on doublet and hose and took the name Fidelio before doing so. She went from prison to prison, seeking to learn the names of the unfortunates behind bars. She drew a blank until she came to an aging jailer whose jail specialized in political prisoners. Rocco had one assistant, Jacquino, and a pretty daughter, Marzelline. When Fidelio applied, Rocco confessed that he could use an extra pair of hands, and engaged him as assistant. He noticed that his daughter Marzelline looked tenderly at the handsome young stripling. Fidelio made 'himself' useful and soon was allowed to help carry meals to the prisoners. Still she found no Florestan. Rocco told of one unfortunate who was kept in a dark underground cell, heavily manacled. Special orders had

been given by the governor of the prison that this man should
be denied all comforts, and that his food ration was to be de-
creased week by week until he died. 'He can't last much longer,
poor fellow,' said Rocco pityingly.

"Fidelio's heart cried, 'It is he!' She pleaded with Rocco to
take her to the dungeon the next time he went. 'No, you're
too tenderhearted,' said the jailer. 'I am hardened to these sights,
and even I can hardly bear to witness his suffering. You are
young, you couldn't endure it.' 'Try me,' said Fidelio. 'See if I
have courage or not.' Inopportunely, the governor, Pizarro,
comes to the prison. He is a real, sneaky, cloak-and-dagger villain. He receives a letter warning him that the King's minister
is coming to inspect the prison. It is imperative that his enemy,
the unfortunate prisoner in solitary confinement, be dispatched
at once. He orders Rocco to see to it. Rocco refuses, murder is
no part of his duties. Pizarro tosses him a bag of gold and
commands that he at least dig the grave—he himself will do the
killing. The gold melts Rocco's resistance, and he assents. As
Pizarro leaves, Fidelio watches him with fear and loathing.
Something evil is afoot, she knows not what. Ever hopeful,
she asks Rocco to allow the prisoners an hour in the courtyard.
It's a beautiful, sunny day, and besides, it's the King's birthday.
Moreover, Fidelio has just been promised the hand of Marzelline,
an unexpected complication, but occasion for a celebration, even
though the marriage will never materialize. Rocco gives her the
keys to the cells and she unlocks them one by one. The
prisoners swarm into the courtyard, taking deep breaths of the
fresh air so long denied them, while Fidelio, hoping against
hope, scans every face, seeking for the one she loves. He is not
among them. Pizarro comes back, harshly orders the prisoners
returned to their cells, and scolds Rocco. He commands him to
perform without delay the task assigned. Doggedly, Rocco takes

pick and shovel, and, with a little urging, permits Fidelio to accompany him.

"They descend to the dungeon where Florestan lies in darkness, dreaming of happier days. Unperceived by him, they set about their grisly task. When they pause in their digging for a cup of wine and a piece of bread, Fidelio gives his portion to the prisoner. In the feeble accents of his thanks, she recognizes the voice of her beloved. It is a heartbreaking moment, for she dares not tell him who she is, and in the darkness he cannot distinguish her features. Nor does he recognize Pizarro, who creeps in with upraised dagger. As he is about to plunge it into his hapless victim, Fidelio throws herself on Florestan's breast, crying, 'I am Leonore, his wife. You will have to kill me first.' And drawing a pistol from her belt, she menaces Pizarro with it. All are breathless—Florestan with joy, Rocco with amazement, Pizarro with frustration, Leonore with determination. Into the moment of silence comes the clear call of a trumpet. It means that the minister is approaching the city. Florestan is saved. He owes his life to Leonore."

When Beethoven finished reading, he wiped his spectacles on a grimy handkerchief, and blew his nose loudly. Schikaneder gave a nod of satisfaction. He knew that Beethoven had rejected thirteen texts. Now he hoped that the luck had turned. He knew—they all knew—that a French opera by Pierre Gaveaux based on Bouilly's play, *Lénore ou l'Amour conjugal* (Leonore, or Conjugal Love), had been given at the Opéra-Comique in Paris five years before. An Italian version, *Leonora ossia L'Amore conjugale,* by Ferdinando Paër, had been given in Dresden. And in another Italian version it appeared as one of over seventy operas composed by the prolific, now almost forgotten Simon Mayr. Such considerations were no deterrent, there being no copyright laws. Each composer treated the subject in his own way; the story was all they had in common. It was unanimously agreed that day that Beethoven should compose an opera based on the story that had so deeply moved him.

Much was to happen before the project materialized. Schikaneder and Baron von Braun had a fight over Mozart's opera *The Magic Flute*. Not only were changes made in Schikaneder's text without his consent, but his name was not even on the program as its author. He seems to have had cause for resentment, but Baron von Braun pulled the rug from under his feet by buying the Theater an der Wien, dismissing Schikaneder, and appointing Josef Sonnleithner to his place as director. Upon Sonnleithner, not Schikaneder, fell the task of writing the German text of *Fidelio, oder Die eheliche Liebe*.

In a letter to Sonnleithner in March 1804, Beethoven begged him to complete the job by June, so that he could get to work on it. Even then, though Beethoven had not yet quarreled with the smooth Baron von Braun, he complained to the librettist, "Ever since we met, his treatment of me has been persistently unfriendly."

There was some reason for this complaint. In Schikaneder's day, Beethoven lived for a time rent-free in rooms above the stage of the Theater an der Wien. Schikaneder knew that Beethoven had a housing problem; his sloppy habits and rudeness antagonized landlords, while his increasing deafness made him suspicious in his dealings with them. Schikaneder believed that living in the smell of grease-paint, free from petty worries, would stimulate his interest in the theatrical world and make him want to compose an opera. But Baron von Braun, not so concerned with the artistic temperament, politely ousted the undesirable tenant when he took over the theater.

Sonnleithner delivered the libretto in June 1804, and Beethoven lost no time. During that summer and the following winter he filled four large notebooks with ideas. In his untidy, almost illegible musical script, he jotted down scraps of melody as they came to his mind. Of the four *Fidelio* notebooks, two have been lost, but the remaining two, now in the Berlin State Library, give evidence of enormous industry. There were no less than eighteen versions of the melody for Florestan's first aria *In des Lebens Frühlingstagen* (In the springtime of life), ten for *Wen ein holdes Weib errungen* (He who has won a noble wife). As for the overture, says Louis Biancolli, in the *Victor Book of the Opera* "the problem . . . so worried Beethoven that he composed, in all, four complete specimens. The first was discarded. The next was used for the world premiere of *Fidelio* in 1805, and is now known as *Leonore Overture No. 2*. The following one—*Leonore Overture No. 3*—was composed for the Viennese revival four months later (February 1805). The one that is now used regularly to open the opera was written for the 1814 revival. It is known simply as the *Overture to Fidelio*."

But we anticipate. When in June 1805 Beethoven betook himself and his notebook to Hetzendorf, he had a mass of chaotic material to be tailored and fitted and organized and orchestrated. Seated in the crotch of an enormous oak tree in the garden of Schönbrunn palace, he scribbled busily. When the going was rough, he strode the garden walks, hands tucked under coattails, handkerchief trailing from pocket, head bent forward, as he has often been pictured. The act of composition was for Beethoven a stormy process, accompanied by shouts, groans, cries of pain or satisfaction. Neighbors listened, fascinated, outside the door of his lodgings when the giant was in labor with a new piece. In the wide spaces of Hetzendorf, he was free to create unheard and unobserved.

By summer's end, the score was in playable shape and he

rounded up a few friends to listen critically. If they had suggestions, they kept them to themselves, knowing that the composer would probably change nothing, whatever their opinion. When Beethoven returned to Vienna, he confidently delivered his score to Josef Sonnleithner and to Baron von Braun. Singers were assigned, rehearsals started. But Beethoven's troubles, far from being over, now really began. To a young soprano, Anna Milder, was given the taxing role of Leonore-Fidelio. He had written the part for her and she had a lovely voice, was willing and anxious. But a mature woman would better have conveyed the emotion of the magnificent arias assigned to her. Even so, she and Luise Müller, who sang Marzelline, were better than the men. The tenor, Demner, was mediocre as Florestan. As for the bass, Sebastian Mayr, who sang Pizarro, he stamped his foot and raged offstage as well as on, declaring loudly that his brother-in-law Mozart would never have written such damn nonsense. He was a conceited little pipsqueak, and Beethoven maliciously complicated his aria *Bald wird sein Blut verrinnen* (Soon his blood will flow) to take him down a peg. In a sea of complaints Beethoven stood like a rock, massive and changeless, no matter how the waves battered. He had moved back to the Theater an der Wien, and was all too accessible.

Not only did the singers complain. He had trouble with the orchestra also. Napoleon was marching into Austria, and, faster than Beethoven could rehearse them, the young players were drafted to defend their country. Beethoven had to train and retrain his men to perform a score that called for painstaking preparation. What good did it do him to write *piano* or *forte* on the parts if the newcomers paid no attention to the markings? One day only two of the three bassoonists showed up. Beethoven was angry, the more so because his patron, Prince von Lobkowitz, had come that day to the rehearsal. The prince couldn't see why the absence of one bassoon should so upset him and ventured to say so. This only made Beethoven angrier. When he passed the prince's palace on his way home, he shook an ungrateful fist at the coat-of-arms over the gate, shouting, "Ass of a Lobkowitz!"

The performance was planned as a celebration of the Empress Maria Theresa's name day, October 15. But the court censors objected to the subject as unsuitable. It took special pleading by Sonnleithner to overcome their objections. He pointed out that Beethoven had spent a year and a half writing the opera, that the Empress had heard the music and found it very beautiful, that the plot had been enacted in the sixteenth century and was not "relevant," that it presented "the quietest description of womanly virtue," that it had created no disturbance in the versions performed in France and Italy, and finally that it was already in rehearsal. The ban was lifted on October 5, too late to give the performance on the date planned, too late to avert the bad luck that dogged the opera.

Napoleon and his army, at war with Austria, occupied Vienna on November 13. The performance of Fidelio was set for November 20. A week before Napoleon marched in, the Empress and her entourage fled the city, leaving the palace of Schönbrunn to Napoleon for headquarters. Most of the nobles and bankers clutched their money boxes and jewels and followed suit. They had heard grisly tales of the efficiency with which the French army plundered occupied cities. Prince von Lobkowitz, Prince Kinsky, and the Archduke Rudolf, the three patrons who paid Beethoven's living expenses, also fled. Worst of all, perhaps, his beloved Josephine von Deym and her two children left Vienna, imploring him to go with them. He refused; how could he desert his opera? By the time they returned, a year later, love had cooled.

On November 20 the opera, which Beethoven entitled *Leonore,* but which the management insisted on calling *Fidelio,* had its premiere. There were few friends in the house to share the composer's opening-night jitters. One compensation, if it can be called so, was that a contingent of French officers showed up, under orders from Napoleon to display this mark of respect for Viennese culture. (He himself did not come.) Nevertheless, the house was barely half full. The Theater an der Wien had opened with great fanfare four years previously. It was the largest and most beautiful in Vienna. Although such modern conveniences as electric footlights and scene-shifting were still in the future, it was spacious and inviting, its blue and silver walls a harmonious background for the blue-coated, white-trousered French officers. There had already been a Beethoven festival in the Theater an der Wien at which his First and Second Symphonies, his Piano Concerto in C minor, and his *Christus am Ölberg* (Christ on the Mount of Olives) had been performed. His first opera deserved a better reception than was accorded it. The French officers, who did not understand German, had no idea of what was happening onstage. They yawned unashamedly behind white-gloved hands. Scattered applause registered no enthusiasm for the dark, bespectacled little man conducting at the piano. At the second performance, Beethoven's friend Stephan von Breuning distributed a poem he had written in praise of opera and composer, but this publicity device failed to stir the public. After three performances, *Fidelio* was withdrawn.

Wasted effort? Not at all, although at the time it may have seemed so. The critic of a leading newspaper, *Der Freimütige* (The Plain Dealer) seemed to think so. He wrote, "The music is far below the expectations which musicians and music lovers justifiably entertained. The melodies as well as the style fail to impress, however earnestly conceived. It cannot be compared with the irresistible emotion which grips us so strongly and uncontrollably in Mozart and Cherubini." J. F. Rochlitz, a highly respected critic, wrote in *Allgemeine musikalische Zeitung* (People's Musical Review), "The whole, appraised thoughtfully and without prejudice, is not remarkable either in inspiration or execution. The Overture consists of a very long Adagio, dragging along in various keys, into which a C major Allegro, also mediocre, is introduced. The arias present no new ideas, they are for the most part too long, the text inordinately repetitious, and to cap the climax, the style remarkably unsatisfactory." No wonder Beethoven wrote that "the whole business of the opera is the most distressing thing in the world."

When his friends returned to Vienna after Napoleon had left, they held an indignation meeting. They declared that this was no way to treat a Beethoven opera. Princess Lichnowsky invited them all to a performance in her music room, at which Beethoven promised to be present. She would play the difficult score on the piano (she had studied with Beethoven), several singers would take part, the violinist Franz Clement would play the melodies on the violin, and Beethoven's brother Kasper, Stephan von Breuning, and others of Beethoven's friends would try to put their finger on the sore spots that the critics had mentioned. It was to be a social event with an underlying purpose.

Everything was done to put Beethoven in a good mood that long evening, which lasted from 7 P.M. until 1 A.M., even to allowing an encore of Florestan's aria, the composer's favorite. At the end the princess' hands fell from the keys, exhausted. She was an invalid, and the effort was great. But she too joined in the discussion that followed. Everyone agreed that the opera was too long, that two or three arias should be cut, and the overture changed. Beethoven roared an emphatic No. The story is that the princess then implored him, for his mother's sake, to reconsider. This touched him. His mother's memory was dear to him. She had done her best, in his unhappy childhood, to protect him from the drunken rages of his ne'er-do-well father. He somberly agreed that his boyhood friend, Stephan von Breuning, should condense the text into two acts, and that the suggested subtractions be made. The princess went to bed, the others trooped into the dining room to celebrate with a midnight supper. Beethoven joined in the gaiety. But his troubles with *Fidelio* were by no means over.

The three acts were reduced to two, the prisoners' chorus and some other numbers shortened, the first act completely re-written. Two performances of this revised version were given, in March and April 1806, with moderate success. But Beethoven was not satisfied. He complained of insufficient rehearsals and errors of singers. He disliked Baron von Braun, with some reason. When he had wished to move back to his rooms in the Theater an der Wien, he had written to Herr Sonnleithner in March 1804, "I know again that if everything depends on the worthy baron's decision, the answer will be No. Well, so be it. I shall never crawl." Now he suspected that the baron was not paying him his due share of the box office receipts. In a stormy scene he accused the baron of short-changing him. The baron said soothingly that there would be more money when the gallery seats as well as the boxes and orchestra were filled. "I don't write for the galleries," Beethoven said scorn-fully, dismissing for the moment his democratic ideals. "My dear Sir, even Mozart didn't disdain to write for the galleries," replied the baron, unruffled. "I want my score back!" Beetho-ven pounded the desk. Without a word, the baron rang a bell, ordered the score brought in, handed it to him, and bowed him out. *Fidelio* was withdrawn from the repertoire.

Beethoven lived to regret it, for the next performances, scheduled for May 1809, rehearsed and ready, had to be canceled. Napoleon bombarded Vienna, Beethoven took refuge from the noise in his brother's cellar with pillows over his ears, the city was again occupied by the French. There was no chance at all for *Fidelio* this time.

Not until May 23, 1814, and not at the Theater an der Wien but at the Kärntnertor Theater, did the opera finally assert itself as the masterpiece it is. The text had been rewritten by Georg Friedrich Treitschke, and the score had again been altered and improved. An excellent cast was thoroughly imbued with the spirit of the music. All went well. Beethoven did, as usual, find one small fly in his ointment in the matter of the customary performance for the composer's benefit, of which he was to receive the total receipts. In the *Wiener Zeitung* (*Vienna News*) he advertised tickets to be sold not at the box office but at his own lodgings. His letter to Archduke Rudolf, his pupil and patron, complained that "The management of the theater is so honest (!) that in spite of its promise it has already performed my opera *Fidelio* without thinking of my benefit. This amiable honesty it would have practiced again had I not been on guard . . . Finally, after considerable exertion on my part, it has been arranged that my benefit of *Fidelio* shall take place on Monday, July 18 . . . To this festival the master humbly invites his exalted pupil and hopes . . . yes, I hope that your Imperial Highness (Rudolf was Empress Maria Theresa's son) will graciously accept and illumine the occasion with your presence . . . It would be nice if your Imperial Highness would try to persuade the other Imperial Highnesses to attend . . .

Your Imperial Highness' faithful and most obedient servant, Ludwig van Beethoven."

This was not an offer of free tickets. His Imperial Highness was one of three patrons who contributed to Beethoven's annuity, but that fact did not entitle him or the others to the privilege of entering without paying. No tickets were given away; however, the house was full, there were many curtain calls, and Beethoven reaped a financial as well as artistic harvest.

While the 1814 text was being revised by Treitschke, Beethoven wrote to him glumly, "I assure you, my dear Treitschke, that this opera will win for me a martyr's crown." Yet a couple of paragraphs later he exulted, "My kingdom is in the air. As the wind often does, so do harmonies whirl around me, and so do things often whirl about too in my soul."

In this same year, 1814, one of the best portraits extant of Beethoven was engraved in steel by a twenty-two-year-old admirer, Blasius Höfel. He was engaged by Beethoven's publisher, Artaria, to make the engraving from a crayon sketch already submitted. Dissatisfied with the likeness, he took it upon himself to ask Beethoven for a sitting. The request was granted, and Höfel appeared eagerly and punctually at the appointed hour. He reckoned without his Beethoven. After sitting for five minutes, the restless composer jumped up, went to the piano, and began to improvise as though he had forgotten Höfel's existence. After waiting for some time, the young man gave up and gathered his materials to leave. Only the timely advent of the servant saved the day. He whispered that if Höfel did his drawing from a seat near the piano while the player was preoccupied, Beethoven would notice nothing. Höfel took this sage advice, and completed his work in only two such sittings. The steel engraving which came out of the sessions became the property of Artaria, a firm which published music by Haydn, Mozart, and Beethoven. It was they who had commissioned the portrait, they who that same year published the first piano version of *Fidelio*.

Since 1814, many famous singers have essayed the leading roles in *Fidelio*. Wilhelmine Schröder-Devrient, known throughout Europe not only on her own account but because of Beethoven's open admiration, made the part of Leonore her own in her great performances at the Kärntnertor Theater in 1822. Beethoven was there the first night. The contralto Marianne Brandt, of a somewhat later vintage, made her American debut at the Metropolitan Opera House as Leonore in 1884 and created a sensation. She had previously sung it in Germany with Albert Niemann as Florestan, whose conception of his role, added to hers, was irresistible. Niemann was her Florestan at the Met when *Fidelio* was again sung there in 1886.

Beautiful Lotte Lehmann fell into the part of Marzelline when she was a young singer in Vienna. She had spent the day of the *Fidelio* performance visiting Beethoven's grave in nearby Währing. When she returned, late in the afternoon, she found a message from the conductor. The Marzelline had a sore throat, was unable to sing, would Lotte substitute? Would she? She did, and was crowned with laurels for her performance. Under similar circumstances she sang Leonore in a later performance when both the principals were taken ill. She became a *Fidelio* expert, and in a preface to the vocal score she stressed the importance of each and every role. She maintained that it contains no "small parts," that Marzelline, her father Rocco, and her lover Jacquino are every bit as vital to an impressive whole as Leonore, Florestan, and Pizarro. The differentiation of character, as embodied in the music, had to be thoughtfully analyzed and displayed if the opera was to achieve maximum effect. The props were also important. Ball and chain must truly clank, no cardboard substitute could be permitted. She relates with gusto one object lesson. In Fidelio's first entrance, he carries a shoulder pack so heavy that he is obviously exhausted and Mar- zelline rushes to take it from him. Rocco gets to him first, takes the heavy shoulder pack and places it on a chair. At the per- formance, Rocco picked it up as though it weighed nothing and tossed it lightly to one side, wholly destroying the effect of Fidelio's panting entrance. Before the next performance, Lotte filled the pack with stones so heavy that she did not need to simulate fatigue, she could hardly carry it. This time, when Rocco picked it up, he almost fell over at the unexpected weight. She never again had to complain that that scene lacked verisimilitude.

THE CAST

Florestan, a Spanish nobleman	*Tenor*
Leonore, his wife (In male attire known as Fidelio)	*Soprano*
Don Fernando, the Prime Minister	*Bass*
Don Pizarro, governor of the prison	*Baritone*
Rocco, chief jailer	*Bass*
Marzelline, his daughter	*Soprano*
Jacquino, his assistant	*Tenor*

Time: Eighteenth century
Place: Seville, Spain
First performance in Vienna, November 20, 1805.

On the principle of saving the best till the last, a discussion of the music of *Fidelio* has been left until now, the story being thoroughly familiar.

ACT I

SCENE I

Jacquino starts the action as he takes advantage of a moment when he and Marzelline are alone together in the jailer's apartment of the gloomy political prison in Seville.

Jetzt, Schätzchen, jetzt sind wir allein (Now, sweetheart, now we are alone) he sings ardently, and begs her to name the day. She puts him off, flirtatiously but firmly. She has long been plighted to him, but as he pleads, she goes off into her own dreams, singing

Oh wär ich schon mit dir vereint (Oh, if only you and I were already united)—and she doesn't mean Jacquino. It is Fidelio she pines for in a passionate outburst, *Die Hoffnung schon erfüllt die Brust* (Hope already overflows in my heart). Leonore disguised as Fidelio enters.

Mir ist so wunderbar (How wonderful it seems), a quartet, shortly ensues. Marzelline's concern for "him" is evident to Rocco and Jacquino. After praising Fidelio for having so well executed his commands, Rocco jovially bestows approval on "him" as a son-in-law. In the quartet, each of the four expresses his feelings at this unexpected turn of events. For Marzelline, it is truly wonderful, and she leads off in a burst of breathless happiness. Fidelio (Leonore) voices dismay but determination to persist in her masquerade, Jacquino jealousy, and Rocco satisfaction. This quartet, a canon imbued with subtle nuance, with voices either alone or exquisitely blended, is one of the wonders of the world of music. When it concludes, the lovers embrace. This can well plunge the mood from the sublime to the

ridiculous, if a fat German soprano, bursting out of her jerkin,
is cast for the part of Fidelio. The embrace, no matter how
chaste, makes the disguise incredible, and the moment hilarious.
But such is grand opera. Hearing is believing, however our eyes
may question. By way of contrast, the quartet is followed by a
bit of rough realism from Rocco.

Hat man nicht auch Gold beineben (If you haven't also a
little gold laid by, so much the worse), he sings. This aria in
praise of money money money has been criticized as "vulgar,"
but money *is* vulgar, so is Rocco, and the sentiments roughly
stated are in keeping with the old man's character.

Ich habe Mut (I have courage) is a trio dominated by
Fidelio. Rocco has told her of one unfortunate prisoner in solitary confinement and she has offered to help care for the poor
wretch. *Gut, Söhnchen, gut, hab' immer Mut* (Good, good, my
son, always keep up your courage) Rocco encourages him, while
Marzelline sighs *Dein gutes Herz wird manchen Schmerz in
diesen Grüften leiden* (Your tender heart will ache painfully
in these gloomy caves). But Fidelio's protestations that "he" is
strong and courageous win Rocco's permission to go along next
time.

SCENE 2

Ha, welch ein Augenblick! (Ha, what a moment!) is a gloating baritone aria sung by Pizarro. Preceded by a march, Pizarro
comes into the prison courtyard with his guard of soldiers.
Rocco brings him the dispatches brought by Fidelio. In one, a
spy informs him that the prime minister will shortly honor the
prison with a surprise visit. The minister believes his friend
Florestan to be dead, so Pizarro must act quickly. The *Augenblick* he so relishes is the moment when he will finish off his

prisoner. His aria concludes *Triumph! Der Sieg ist mein!* (Triumph! Victory is mine!) Peremptorily, he orders his guards to patrol the streets leading to the prison. He sends a trumpeter to watch from the prison rampart, with instructions to blow a fanfare the minute he sees the minister's party approaching the gates. He then summons Rocco, who has hidden uneasily while all this was going on. *Jetzt, Alter, alter, jetzt hat es Eile!* (Now, old man, now, there's no time to lose!) he tells him brusquely. Rocco must kill the prisoner. Rocco demurs, but finally, tempted by a bag of gold pieces, he agrees to become an accessory before the fact, and at least to dig a grave in an old cistern in the prisoner's cell. Pizarro will himself do the killing, and without further ado he makes his exit to see that his orders are carried out to the letter.

Abscheulicher! Wo eilst du hin? Was hast du vor in wilden Grimme? (Vile creature, where are you hurrying? What have you planned in your wild rage?) sings Fidelio, who has been lurking nearby. "He" has heard enough to be very uneasy. "He" shakes his fist at the retreating figure as "he" vents his rage and frustration in this impassioned, unforgettably dramatic aria. In it, anger is succeeded by despair, and finally by the return of hope and determination. To lighten the gloom, a brief scene ensues between Marzelline and Jacquino in which he again beseeches her to name the day. She asks Rocco to assure him that there won't be any day, and goes with her father to obtain Pizarro's consent to her marriage with Fidelio. When they return, Fidelio prevails upon Rocco to allow the prisoners to leave their cells and walk in the courtyard. "He" still cherishes the hope that Florestan may be among them. Marzelline joins in the plea, the cells are unlocked, the prisoners flock into the courtyard.

O welche Lust! (O what joy to bathe in the sunshine!) The murmur of the prisoners' chorus swells to a rapturous outcry.

Fidelio goes from one to another, but in vain; the one "he" seeks is not among them. The abrupt return of Pizarro, and his sharp command to return the prisoners to their cells, quells the joyous outburst. Reminded of the grisly task that must be done at once, Rocco shoulders his spade. Fidelio insists on going with him, and as the curtain falls they are about to descend to the dungeon.

ACT II

SCENE I

Gott! Welch' Dunkel hier! O grauenvolle Stille! (God, what darkness here! O menacing silence!) Florestan laments, as he sits shackled on a rock and chained to the dungeon wall. An anecdote is told of one misdirected Florestan who clutched his head with his manacled hand as he exclaimed, "What darkness here!" The audience laughed. But Florestan's plight is no laughing matter. His plaint tapers off to a note of resignation, and then, half-delirious, he plunges into an aria reminiscent of happier days:

In des Lebens Frühlingstagen (In the springtime of life). This is the aria that Beethoven wrote and rewrote, perhaps trying to recapture in song the days of his own young manhood when deafness had not yet become his jailer. It changes its mood from pleasurable reminiscence to the thought of impending death, and Florestan has a vision of Leonore leading him to heaven. The aria is long. It is no wonder that he falls into exhausted slumber at the end. This gives Rocco and Fidelio their opportunity to dig unperceived. They come down the steps at the rear, Rocco guiding them with a lantern, and set to work at once. Their duet, *Nur hurtig fort, nur frisch gegraben* (Come,

come, dig!), is half-spoken, half-sung. Fidelio goes fearfully to peer at the sleeping prisoner but in the darkness cannot discern his features. Rocco reproves him, calling him back to dig. When Rocco stops for a drink from a jug of wine, Fidelio begs to be allowed to give a swallow, and also some bread, to the prisoner, who has awakened. The last meal of the condemned man! What difference can it make? Rocco too is sorry for the prisoner, and assents.

O Dank dir, Dank! O Dank! O Dank! O Dank! Euch, euch werde Lohn in bessern Welten (Oh thank you, thanks! Oh thanks! Oh thanks! Oh thanks! You'll be rewarded in a better world!) sings Florestan movingly. *Gott, diese Stimme!* (God, that voice!) whispers Fidelio. She murmurs words of encouragement. Rocco sings of his regret, joining Florestan and Fidelio in a trio of wondrous beauty. But Rocco dares not forget the call of duty; he goes to give the signal that all is prepared. Enter now the villain, Pizarro.

Er sterbe! Doch er soll erst wissen, wer ihm sein stolzes Herz zerfleischt (He shall die! But first he shall know who it is that pierces his proud heart). Pizarro orders Fidelio to withdraw and the prisoner freed from the wall. He advances upon Florestan with a dagger. In the operatic tradition, he delays striking the fatal blow until he has sung a long aria revealing his name and gloating in triumph. This gives Fidelio "his" opportunity. "He" has hidden in the darkness and now rushes out to stand between victim and killer, crying, "I am Leonore his wife, first you must kill me." Pizarro is nonplussed, Florestan is overcome, Rocco amazed. By the time Pizarro has recovered sufficiently to advance again upon husband and wife, Leonore has drawn a pistol from her belt and holds him at bay. In the silence a trumpet fanfare sounds. The minister! Waves of thankful music flow from the orchestra dropping "like the gentle rain from heaven" upon the ears beneath. This ineffable climax comprises the emotional sum total of the opera; it holds the audience enthralled. Some conductors insert Overture No. 3 here. It sounds eminently right in this spot, where it can fully be savored while the situation sinks in. Then Jacquino calls from the head of the stairs that Don Fernando is there. A revealing quartet ensues:

Es schlägt der Rache Stunde! Du sollst gerettet sein! (The hour for revenge has struck! You shall be saved!) sings Leonore, and Florestan weakly agrees, "I shall be saved," while Pizarro curses, and Rocco wonders what will happen next. Pizarro and Rocco hasten to the courtyard to greet the minister, leaving Leonore and Florestan alone together.

O namenlose Freude! (O inexpressible joy!) *O meine Leonore, was hast du für mich getan?* (Oh my Leonore, what have you done for my sake?) he marvels, and she soothes him, *Nichts, nichts, mein Florestan* (Nothing, nothing, my Florestan). They fall into each other's arms. Rocco returns and bids them come with him. Don Fernando has ordered that all the prisoners be brought out into the courtyard. They move slowly to the stairs leading to freedom, each supporting the other.

SCENE 2

In the sunny courtyard of the prison, nobles, townsfolk, even children, have gathered to welcome Don Fernando, the prime minister. The prisoners have been released from their cells and kneeling, await his words.

Heil sei dem Tag, Heil sei der Stunde (Hail to the day, hail to the hour) they sing in chorus.

Des besten Königs Wink und Wille führt mich zu euch, ihr Armen, her (The wish and command of the best of kings brings me to you, you poor creatures) is Don Fernando's message. He bids the prisoners rise from their knees, they are free. Leonore and Florestan have emerged from the dungeon. Don Fernando is astounded and overjoyed to see Florestan, the friend whom he has believed dead. Rocco is emboldened to relate the misdeeds of Pizarro, who is led away to be punished. Don Fernando orders Rocco to strike off Florestan's shackles but then he reconsiders, and allows Leonore to set her husband free.

O Gott! O welch ein Augenblick! (Oh God! Oh, what a moment!) sing the chorus and principals. All the prisoners are released.

Wer ein holdes Weib errungen, stimm' in unsern Jubel ein (Whoever has won a noble wife come join our celebration) is the grand finale in which the chorus leads off. Florestan thankfully echoes, *Wer ein* solches *Weib errungen* (Whoever has won *such* a wife), and Leonore explains, *Liebe führte mein Bestreben* (Love guided my efforts). Marzelline, Jacquino, and Don Fernando swell the chorus of *Wer ein solches Weib errungen*. A sisterly kiss from Leonore reconciles Marzelline to marriage with Jacquino and the curtain falls on a scene of bliss, in joyous contrast to the previous gloom. Virtue has triumphed.

"As a drama and as an opera, *Fidelio* stands almost alone in its perfect purity, in the moral grandeur of its subject, and in the resplendent ideality of its music," wrote George Upton. Beethoven himself commented wryly, "Of all my children, *Fidelio* is the one that brought me the most sorrow, and for that reason it is the one most dear to me." It has been this writer's privilege to hear *Fidelio* frequently, in performances ranging from opera workshop to Theater an der Wien to the Metropolitan Opera House in New York. Never has it failed to evoke the instantaneous, heartfelt emotions induced by the drama and by Beethoven's incomparable music.

RECORDINGS*

Dernesch, Donath, Vickers, Kélémen, Ridderbusch, Karajan, Berlin
    Phil. & Deutsche Oper Cho.   3-Angel S-3773

Jones, Mathis, King, Schreier, Talvela, Adam, Crass, Böhm, Dresden
    St. Op.   3-Deutsche Grammophon 2709031. 3-DG 2720009;
          6-DG 3378–011 (cassette tape) ("Beethoven Edition")

Kuchta, Patzak, Rehfuss, Bamberger, N. German Radio Orch. &
    Cho.   2-Nonesuch 73005

Ludwig, Vickers, Frick, Berry, Klemperer, Phil. Orch. & Cho.
          3-Angel S-3625

Excerpts from above   Angel S-36168

Nilsson, McCracken, Krause, Prey, Böhme, Maazel, Vienna Phil.
          2-London 1259

Excerpts from above   London 26009

Rysanek, Haefliger, Fischer-Dieskau, Seefried, Fricsay (selections)
          Deutsche Grammophon 922-020 (cassette tape)

Bampton, Peerce, Toscanini   2-RCA LM-6025

Mödl, Jurinac, Windgassen, Edelmann, Frick, Schock, Furtwängler,
    Vienna Phil. & St. Op. Cho.   3-Seraphim 6022

* Taken from Schwann-1 Record & Tape Guide, February 1973, and
from Schwann-2 Record & Tape Guide, Spring 1973.

Verdi's

AÏDA

VERDI'S

Aïda

VERDI'S *AÏDA*
THREE-RING SPECTACULAR
SEE AND HEAR *AÏDA*
LIVE ELEPHANTS, EGYPTIAN DANCING GIRLS
ROYAL KHEDIVE NILE BAND!
COME ONE, COME ALL!

This is the way Verdi's grand opera *Aïda* could have been advertised if a special effort were needed to attract an audience, and if the Ringling Brothers had produced it. But it was a smash hit from the beginning. The regulation billboards are all that is needed to inform the public of the treat in store. They read:

AÏDA

Grand Opera by Giuseppe Verdi

CAST

The King of Egypt	Bass
Amneris, his daughter	Mezzo-soprano
Amonasro, King of Ethiopia	Baritone
Aïda, his daughter and slave of Amneris	Soprano

Radames, an Egyptian officer   *Tenor*
Ramfis, High Priest of Egypt   *Bass*
A Messenger   *Tenor*
Priestess   *Soprano*

Time: period of the Pharaohs' power
Place: Memphis and Thebes
First performance at Cairo, December 24, 1871.

Despite the circus features, Aïda was a serious opera. Freedom was its theme, one for which Verdi was already famous.

For Verdi, freedom was threefold—political, personal, and artistic. He knew that in the Egypt of the Pharaohs in which his opera Aïda was set, conquered peoples were enslaved as a matter of course, however loudly they cried the equivalent of "We shall overcome." And slavery was something which Verdi could not tolerate, particularly the brand of slavery which existed in the United States, to be legally abolished after the Civil War, ten years before the first performance of Aïda.

Verdi believed in absolute artistic liberty, not only the right to write his music whatever way he chose, but also in his right to use his operas to plead in music for any form of freedom he chose. In Nabucco, his first successful opera, produced in Milan, 1842, the theme is the conquest of Jerusalem by King Nebuchadnezzar, the enslavement and exile of the Jews, their longing for freedom and their eventual release after the death of the wicked king.

In Aïda, years later, he sings of a conquered Ethiopian princess exiled to Egypt. The Egyptians worship alien Gods and perform alien rituals. She has the misfortune to fall in love with Radames, who has led the army that defeated her people in a bloody battle. To complicate the situation, she has been given as a slave to the Egyptian princess Amneris, who wants Radames for herself. The story is not only about the conflict between patriotism and love, but about the right of all people to be free. Verdi is obviously on the side of Aïda and freedom. He depicts her as gentle, loving, suffering, selfless, loyal, and enduring, while Amneris, her rival, is vain, jealous, wily, cruel, and inclined to exercise power without mercy. Radames is a bit of a weakling caught between two strong forces, neither of which he wholly comprehends.

There is no better way to follow the story of *Aïda*, barring a live performance, than seated beside a record player, libretto in one hand, and a list of especially notable arias in the other. There are many recordings of the entire opera from which to choose. I have quoted first lines of special favorites as they occur in the story in the original language, to make them easier to find. The translations are not literal, nor do they stick to musical phrasing at the expense of meaning, as many others do. They are as colloquial as I dare make them without irreverence.

THE STORY

ACT I

SCENE I

A hall in the palace of the King of Egypt affords a glimpse through a window toward the Pyramids in the distance and the palaces and temples of the capital city of Memphis. Within the hall, the white-robed High Priest, Ramfis, confers with Radames, a gallant young captain of the Egyptian guard. Ramfis reports a rumor that the neighboring country of Ethiopia,

recently subjugated, is again on the warpath, laying siege to the
proud city of Thebes. At that very moment a messenger is expected with the latest news. A commander must be appointed
to lead the Egyptian army; the question is, who shall it be?

"Have you consulted the Goddess Isis?" asks Radames re-
spectfully, for over all of Egypt broods the shadow of the Gods,
whose word is law.

"I have," replies Ramfis, "and she has indicated that it must
be a man who is young, loyal, and willing to serve." He looks
significantly at Radames, who seizes exultantly on the gentle
hint. Radames starts to fantasize in song on the possibility that
he will be chosen. He will fight and conquer, and return to lay
his laurels at the feet of his beloved Aïda. He seems to forget that
Aïda is an Ethiopian, an enemy made prisoner during the last
battle who may not relish a lover who again leads the attack
upon her country. With a degree of military insensitivity, he
sings of his determination to demand her freedom and her return to her native land as the guerdon of victory. At the very
thought, he bursts into a rapturous love song, Celeste Aïda (My
heavenly Aïda!). This is an aria that even the tone-deaf hum
as they leave the opera house, not alone because of its compelling
melody and its ardor, but because the theme reappears later in
the opera.

Aïda is the slave of the King's daughter, Amneris. As she goes
humbly about her tasks, nobody suspects that she is a princess
in her own right, the daughter of the Ethiopian King Amonasro.
But Amneris has noticed the exchange of tender glances between
Aïda and Radames and suspects their feeling for each other.
She is determined to have Radames for her own. Scornfully
she assures herself that he would not stoop so low as to prefer
a slave; nevertheless, she vows to learn the truth.

As the last notes of Celeste Aïda die away, Amneris comes

upon Radames. She sings *Quale insolita gioia nel tuo sguardo!* (How unusually happy you look!), and asks the reason. He confides his hope of military glory, but she coyly asks if there is no other reason, perhaps love of woman rather than love of battle that so rejoices him. He is alarmed, fearing that he may have given her some sign of his love for Aïda. As he utters a cry, *"Dessa"* (She is here), Aïda, looking mournful, enters. Amneris, watching jealously, finds her suspicion heightened. She utters her resentment in a bitter aside, while Radames and Aïda separately voice their fears of her jealousy. *Vieni, o diletta* (Come, dearest friend) sings Amneris hypocritically to Aïda. "Tell me your troubles, you can trust me." Aïda admits only that she is distressed at the strife between Egypt and Ethiopia, but Amneris draws her own conclusions.

With pomp and ceremony the King, the High Priest, ministers, and army officers enter, to a fanfare from the orchestra. The King sings *Alta cagion v'aduna* (A mighty cause brings you to rally round your king). A breathless messenger enters. He announces that an Ethiopian force led by King Amonasro has invaded the sacred soil of Egypt. The enemy, says the messenger, is advancing on neighboring Thebes. Unanimously, all cry, *Guerra! Guerra!* (War! War!), Radames loudest of all. The High Priest announces that Isis has decreed that Radames is to lead the Egyptian army.

Radames! Aïda trembles. This means her beloved will fight against her father. For whom shall she pray? For an Egyptian victory, which spells defeat for her countrymen? For her countrymen, who will rob her of her love? Her conflict is deeply personal, yet symbolic of the struggle between generations, races, and civilizations. Her somber undercurrent of comment on old and young, father and lover, provides a foil to the shouts of *Guerra! Guerra! Vittoria!* which resound.

Su! del Nilo al sacro lido (Up! On the sacred banks of the Nile protect your country) sings the King, and leads the way to the Temple of Phtah, the Egyptian God of War. All except Aïda follow him into the temple singing lustily, *Ritorna vincitor* (Return victorious).

Alone, Aïda gives way to despair in a great emotional aria, *Ritorna vincitor!* (Return victorious indeed!) she echoes. "Never was heart torn by such cruel agony. The sacred names of my father, my lover, I dare not speak aloud, nor even remember." Sarcastically, she repeats *Ritorna vincitor* and bursts into an urgent appeal to the Gods for pity. *Numi, pietà* (Gods, have pity) she sings. This is an aria of intense feeling, one of the most beautiful of the opera. So eloquently does she plead for divine intervention it would seem that the most stony-hearted Gods would have to take pity. Alas, no! Aïda is predestined to sorrow.

SCENE 2

The scene changes to the interior of the Temple of Phtah. Through clouds of incense, the figure of the High Priest Ramfis is discerned at the altar. He invokes the blessing of the Gods on the battle to come, and the High Priestess joins her voice to his. The sacred chant, *Immenso, immenso Phtah* (Mighty, mighty Phtah) is rich in Oriental color. Here Verdi employed intervals peculiar to the East, and themes which sound as though they had come direct from an ancient temple. This creates a piquantly exotic atmosphere that transports the audience to Pharaoh's Egypt. The solemn dance which the priestesses execute as they chant adds to the hypnotic power of the scene. Now Radames, unarmed, approaches the altar. He bows his head to be crowned with the silver veil of authority, a symbolic sword is placed in his hand, and his voice joins the others in a prayer for victory.

This is the Grand Consecration scene, and it is both grand and consecrated. Again, Radames gives no sign of concern for his beloved. He is a soldier first, a lover, second. Gratefully, loyally, in all sincerity, he joins the High Priest and the chorus in a powerful prayer, *Nume, custode e vindice* (God, guardian and protector of this sacred land, hear us!). On a surge of sound, the act ends.

ACT II

SCENE I

A bloody battle has been fought. The victorious Egyptian army is about to return in triumph. Amneris, before a mirror, prinks, and her slaves dance and sing as they prepare her for the festivities that will greet the hero, Radames. She passionately proclaims her love for him and her joy in his victory as she sings *Vieni, amor mio* (Come, my love). But her eyes darken as they fall on Aïda, and suspicion again plagues her. Determined to learn the truth, she calls Aïda to her side with honeyed words. "Why so sad, my dear?" she asks. *Fu la sorte dell'armi a' tuoi funesta* (It was the fortunes of war that your side lost).

"How can I be happy, uncertain of my fate, of my father's fate?" counters Aïda.

"There's always love to console you," Amneris suggests slyly. Aïda's change of expression, and her unguarded reply, *Amore, amore! Gaudio, tormento* (Love, love, joy, torment), do nothing to allay Amneris' suspicions. Cunningly she continues her professions of friendship until Aïda almost believes them. Then, with cruel determination to ascertain the whole truth, Amneris breaks the false news that Radames has been killed in action. No Sherlock Holmes is needed to deduce from Aïda's reaction that she loves Radames. She utters an involuntary cry of grief and almost faints. "Aha!" gloats Amneris. "You love him!" Maliciously she reveals that she has lied, that Radames still lives and that she intends to have him for her own, that she will tolerate no rival. Aïda makes a futile gesture of defiance, then falls at her mistress' feet begging for mercy. She pleads in vain. *Trema, vil schiava* (Tremble, vile slave), thunders Amneris. She humiliates Aïda to the depths with a command to remain beside her as the lowliest of her slaves during the festivities, and threatens to have her killed without mercy if she rebels. Aïda calls on the Gods for pity, *Numi pietà* (Gods, have pity). She surely needs divine help, for no human help is forthcoming. Sadly she follows her resplendent mistress to the square where the Big Scene takes place, the triumphant return of the victorious Egyptian army.

SCENE 2

The King, the High Priest, and the retinue enter. The King ascends the throne and Amneris in glittering raiment takes her place beside him. Aïda lurks in the shadows. A great crowd awaits the parade. *Gloria all'Egitto* (Glory to Egypt) resounds from all throats in a chorus that raises the roof. The rejoicing has no bounds. The famous march is introduced in a tingling orchestral interlude which precedes the parade of the victors. With rhythmic elation, the army and their spoils of war—banners, dancing girls, captured chariots, images of the Gods—pass before the reviewing stand to the strains of the march.

After a chorus of thanks and Glorias, and an invitation,

Vieni, o guerriero vindice (Come, O conquering hero!), Radames enters. The hero kneels before the King, who sings *Salvator
della patria* (Savior of your country, I salute you). The King calls
him "my son" and hands Amneris the triumphal wreath, which
she places on Radames' head. The King, in a transport of joy,
promises to grant him any wish he expresses. Radames asks that
the prisoners be brought in. He intends to ask for their pardon
and release, and, at the same time, for Aïda's. Among those
captured is Amonasro, the Ethiopian King. Aïda's horrified *Mio
padre!* (My father!) is heard by all, but no one recognizes
in the battered warrior the King.

   With a warning sign to her not to betray him, Amonasro steps
forward as spokesman for the group. Eloquently he describes
the death in battle of King Amonasro, and argues that, the King
being dead, there is nothing now to be feared from the Ethiopians. The High Priest disagrees. He urges the King to harden
his heart, to put all enemies of Egypt to the sword, and the
people agree. They shout for death in a powerful chorus. Aïda
prays for mercy, Ramfis sings of revenge, Radames gazes with
pity on Aïda's tortured visage. At last he takes notice! Finally
the King, reminded of his pledge, agrees to free the prisoners,
but as a concession to the High Priest he holds Aïda and her
father as hostages. This being settled, he makes a further magnificent gesture and promises Radames the hand of Amneris and
that one day he shall rule over Egypt. Amneris gloats, Aïda
despairs, Radames is stunned. This is not what he intended at
all. Amonasro fiercely whispers to Aïda to take heart, that in
time she may find herself the savior of her people. The chorus,
Gloria, gloria all'Egitto (Glory, glory to Egypt), drowns all
other voices and Act II ends brilliantly on this chorus and a
stirring repetition of the March.

ACT III

While Radames is being wined and dined in the boring routine reserved for celebrities, the curtain remains mercifully down. It rises on a moonlit, starlit grotto, the silvery sheen of the Nile reflecting moon and stars, the Temple of Isis in the rear. From the Temple, voices ask the blessing of Isis on Amneris' marriage, singing, *Oh tu che sei d'Osiride madre immortale e sposa . . . soccorri, soccorri, a noi pietosa* (Oh Thou who to Osiris art wife and mother immortal, succor us!). The High Priest and Amneris, who is closely veiled and guarded, approach the Temple from a boat on the Nile. Amneris is to be married the next day and the High Priest accompanies her to the Temple for rest, meditation, and prayer.

Hardly have they entered its portals than Aïda appears, also veiled. She has promised to meet Radames in this romantic spot for a last farewell. While she awaits him, she sings nostalgically of Ethiopia, which she will never see again, in a great aria: *O patria mia, mai più, mai più ti rivedrò!* (O, my country, never again, never again shall I behold thee!)

A figure advances into the moonlight. *Ciel, mio padre!* (Heavens, my father!) exclaims Aïda. Amonasro is the last person she wants to see at this moment. What girl, meeting her boy friend, welcomes her father instead? Besides, she knows his refrain of "We will overcome," his ruthless pursuit of revenge. Love, not hate, is her own motif. But Amonasro gives her no choice. In a magnificent duet, he plays on her love for Radames and her resentment against Amneris to evoke her built-in loyalty to her father, her country, and her freedom, *Rivedrai le foreste imbalsamate* (Again you'll behold our fragrant forests). He depicts to her in glowing terms the joy of returning as a princess to her native land, where she will live happily forever after with Radames to share her throne, if only . . . If only what? She shrinks, but allows herself to dwell fondly on the prospect until he brings her up short. The remnants of the Ethiopian army, he says, plan a surprise attack on the Egyptian army within a few days. He knows all the Egyptians' plans except the route they will take. He intends to waylay them, but in order to do so he must know where to attack. He orders her, when Radames comes, to extract the information from him. At first she recoils in horror and refuses outright. But Amonasro will not take no for an answer. He depicts the carnage of Ethiopians should the Egyptians again defeat them and, when she still refuses, he summons the ghost of her mother to curse her. Begging for mercy, Aïda falls to her knees, imploring him to lift the curse. He is pitiless. Loyalty to him, to her people, to her country must take precedence over all other claims, he reiterates. *O patria, o patria, quanto mi costi!* (O my country, o my country, how dearly you cost me!) she grieves as she crumples into unwilling compliance.

"Courage!" cries Amonasro, well satisfied, and hastens to conceal himself behind the palm trees to eavesdrop. This is a magnificently dramatic duet.

His savagery contrasts strongly with the mild transports of Radames, who now approaches. *Pur ti riveggo, mia dolce Aïda* (Again I behold you, my dearest Aïda), he sings. When he professes undying affection, she asks coldly how he plans to deal with the triple threat of King, Amneris, and priests, all of whom are against her. He replies that once he has again beaten the Ethiopians—of which happy outcome there is no doubt in his mind—he will prostrate himself before the King and ask for Aïda to wife. "And what will Amneris be doing? You may be

sure that she will see to it that my father and I die. No, no, we
must flee, that is the only way out." And with impulsive
warmth, she sings seductively, *Fuggiam gli ardori inospiti* (Let's
flee this hostile land). She goes on to picture a Utopia where
they will live together in a state of perpetual euphoria. He is
aghast at the thought of flight. How can she ask him to desert
the country to which he has devoted his life, for which he has
fought and bled; the country where he first saw her, Aïda, his
dearly beloved?

Like any normal woman, Aïda retorts, "No? You won't?
Then you don't really love me. Go! Go to your Amneris. Leave
me and my father to our fate!" Radames weakens. *Ah no!
Fuggiamo!* (Ah, no, let's flee) he says. Their rapturous voices
blend in duet, one of the few nonmilitary happy moments in the
opera, picturing the paradise that awaits them. As they take the
first steps toward flight, Aïda pauses suddenly. "What road must
we take if we are to avoid the Egyptian army?" she asks ingen-
uously.

"The gorge of Napata," the unsuspecting Radames replies.

"That's where I will post my army!" cries Amonasro from the
shadows.

"Who speaks?" Radames halts, shocked. Amonasro steps into
the moonlight.

"Aïda's father, and the King of the Ethiopians," he replies.

Radames, incredulous, voices his shock. *Io son disonorato . . .*
(I am undone . . .) cries Radames. From the Temple of Isis
comes another cry, *Traditor!* (Traitor!), from Amneris, as she,
and the High Priest, and others rush out. Amonasro attempts to
stab Amneris, but Radames intervenes. The High Priest calls
the guards. *Presto! Fuggite!* (Hasten! Flee!), Radames urges
Aïda and Amonasro. Amonasro drags Aïda away half-fainting.

"Priest, I remain with you," sings Radames, as he turns himself over to the High Priest.

ACT IV

It is the day of judgment for Radames. In the hall through which he must pass to the judgment chamber, Amneris crouches, weeping. She knows that treason is punishable by death, that Radames is a traitor and must die. But she loves him still. Agony at the thought of losing him contends with jealousy. If only he will promise to return her love, she vows to have him pardoned *L'abborrita rivale a me sfuggia* (My hated rival still escapes me). She debates with herself in a moving recitative, and commands the guards to bring Radames to her before taking him to his judges. *Già i sacerdoti adunansi* (The priests are already assembling), she sings to him. This is her big scene. Passionately she implores him to clear himself, to live for her sake. Coldly he reminds her that he was willing to sacrifice his country, his honor, his life, his all, for love of Aïda. At this, her fury of jealousy flames anew. He accuses her of having murdered Aïda. No, she replies, Amonasro was killed in the battle at the gorge of Napata, and his army was routed, but Aïda vanished and is probably still alive. Let him but promise never again to see Aïda, and she, Amneris, will forgive all and will intercede with the priests. In a recitative, *Or, s'io ti salvo, giurami che più non la vedrai* (But if I save you, swear that you'll never see her again), she makes her point.

He refuses, and romantically proclaims undying devotion to his own true love. His fate is sealed. She watches numbly as guards lead him away, and sings her despair, *Oh! chi lo salva?* (Oh, who will save him?).

The priests enter and go to Radames' prison, where they pray for guidance, *Spirito del Nume, sovra noi discendi!* (Eternal spirit, descend upon us!). It is the priests who influence people and events. It is they who selected Radames to lead the Egyptian hosts, they who determined that Aïda and Amonasro should be held hostage, they to whom the infidel Aïda and the pious Amneris alike turned for help. It is now they who sit in judgment on the offender, and mete out his punishment.

Radames stands with bowed head before his judges. Ramfis solemnly calls upon him to speak in his own defense. He is silent. Three times he is exhorted to speak. Three times he refuses. Amneris prays aloud, but the chorus shouts "Traitor!" drowning her prayer. Radames' silence is construed as an admission of guilt. He is sentenced to be buried alive, execution to take place at once.

As the priests leave the judgment hall, Amneris clutches the hem of their garments, entreating them to show mercy. All in vain! Louder than ever the populace shout *Traditor! Traditor!* (Traitor! Traitor!), a veritable cry for execution. Amneris curses the priests in a frenzied outburst, and rushes wildly away as the curtain falls.

The last scene shows the interior of the Temple of Phtah, in two sections. Above is the altar, around which gather priests and priestesses; below is the subterranean vault, Radames' death chamber. He is put into it, a massive stone is placed over the entrance, and he is left to his fate. *La fatal pietra sovra me si chiuse* (The fatal stone above me is closing) he sings, and mourns that nevermore will he see the light of day nor behold his beloved Aïda. *Aïda, ove sei tu?* (Aïda, where art thou?) he cries aloud. He has not long to wait for an answer. A form materializes in the darkness. He believes that he is seeing things, that the ghost of Aïda has come to haunt him. But she answers, *Son io* (It is I), and assures him that she is very much alive and has come to share the doom she has brought upon him. He is incredulous, wretched, and happy, all at the same time. In anticipation of his sentence, she had crept into the tomb and hidden, awaiting his coming.

He pleads with her not to make such a sacrifice, she so young, so pure, so beautiful. He tries to lift the stone that seals them so that she may escape, but he cannot budge it. Finally, clasped in each other's arms, they await death. The priests and priestesses above intone a dirge, a somber accompaniment to the lovers' final duet, *O terra addio* (O earth, farewell). Amneris, prostrate on the stone which seals the vault, prays for eternal peace for Radames, as Aïda dies.

By the time the curtain falls, the audience has identified so completely with the emotionally torn principals that the ultimate tragedy becomes a personal one. The music is responsible, for it portrays with rare clarity the internal struggle of each individual as external events unfold. Choruses and triumphs, ritual and splendor, on the one hand; and on the other, human beings: an unscrupulous, ambitious father, a daughter torn between love and duty, a young man bewitched and bewildered, a woman made wicked by overweening jealousy, a High Priest fanatically possessed by his Gods. The alternation of melodious aria with exclamatory chorus, the deliberate curtailment of recitative, the harmonious duets and trios, add up to an opera of irresistible impact.

Critics agree unanimously that *Aïda* not only marked a significant change in Verdi's style of writing, but gave a new direction to Italian opera. In the eighteenth century the Italian model by Mozart in Vienna, by George Frederick Handel and Johann Christian Bach in London, and, in the first half of the nine-

teenth century, by Gioacchino Rossini in Paris, prevailed. Verdi
continued in their tradition, but with *Aïda* he went a step further. In his Introduction to the vocal score of *Aïda* the critic
W. J. Henderson wrote: "In *Aïda* he (Verdi) has abandoned
the elementary dance rhythms, the antique melodic formula, the
bald and empty passages of recitative between the set numbers, and the cheap and noisy instrumentation. The rhythms
are broader and more scholarly; the melody is fresh, original
and diversified in character; the harmony is immensely rich and
expressive, and the instrumentation glows with Oriental warmth
and color . . . While Verdi continued to employ the set forms,
the aria, duet, trio, etc., he molded them on broader lines and in-
fused into them a truer dramatic utterance . . . In a word, he
showed how a man of genius could vitalize the shopworn ap-
paratus of Italian grand opera, just as Mozart had done nearly a
century earlier in his *Don Giovanni.*"

Ten years before *Aïda,* Verdi's opera *Un Ballo in maschera*
(A Masked Ball) drove him into the revolutionary tide of Italian
politics. "Italy for the Italians" was the popular battle cry when
he was a young man. *Un Ballo in maschera* was an opera which
echoed that cry.

The opera was commissioned by Ferdinand II, King of the
Two Sicilies, which included Sicily and Naples, and the people
of Naples longed to depose this unpopular monarch. He was a
grotesque, cruel, despotic ruler whom they nicknamed *La
Bomba* (The Bomb) because he had bombarded cities in Sicily
during an insurrection. They wanted Naples united with the
provinces of Piedmont and Savoy as one Italy, under King
Victor Emmanuel. Verdi was wholeheartedly in sympathy with
these freedom-seekers and against their tyrannical ruler. It so
happened that *Un Ballo in maschera*—which was originally
titled *Gustavo III*—was based on the true story of the murder

of a king—Gustav III of Sweden—at a masked ball in the eighteenth century. Immediately before Verdi was to go to Naples to supervise rehearsals, word reached Italy that an Italian in Paris had attempted to kill Emperor Napoleon III. Napoleon narrowly escaped with his life, and every noble in every kingdom in Europe trembled for his own. Since Italy was rife with revolution, La Bomba shook in his boots. He would have liked to close the city gates to all outsiders. He was already having trouble keeping his rebellious subjects in check. The plot of Verdi's *Gustavo III* had been accepted by the court censors, the contract had been signed, rehearsals held. Then La Bomba decreed that it should not be performed, on the ground that it was subversive and dangerous to safety—his safety. On the very eve of the performance, he forbade it. Not only this, he commanded Verdi to leave the city at once and sent an officer to escort him to the border. But Verdi insisted on his right to hold Naples to its contract. La Bomba hysterically ordered his arrest. But no one, not even the police, would touch a hair of Verdi's head. On the contrary, wherever he went he was protected. Friends surrounded him and prevented such suspicious characters as policemen or soldiers from coming near him. The walls of Naples were scrawled in red, green, and black chalk, the colors of Victor Emmanuel's flag, with the words "Viva Verdi." The letters of Verdi's name, duly capitalized, also stood for Victor Emmanuel, Re d'Italia, and thus were doubly symbolic of freedom, political and artistic. "Viva Verdi" decorated the walls of Rome also, where a large segment of the Roman population sought to escape the domination of the Pope, as Naples did that of La Bomba.

Despite popular backing, *Gustavo III* was not performed in Naples. In order to avoid violence, Verdi finally agreed to substitute *Simon Boccanegra*, an opera on a less questionable subject. He arranged to have *Gustavo III* premiered in Rome the following season. The setting of the opera was switched from eighteenth-century Stockholm to seventeenth-century Boston and the character King Gustav III of Sweden changed to Riccardo, a colonial governor. The opera was now called *Un Ballo in maschera*. It was welcomed enthusiastically and in Rome no crowned heads fell because of it.

Meanwhile, Verdi retired to his farm in Sant' Agata to watch political developments. Victor Emmanuel's prime minister, Count Camillo di Cavour, was his great friend. Cavour, hoping that the various states would unite in the battle for freedom, had deliberately provoked the Austrians into attacking Italy. Verdi sympathized, and with his own money bought guns and ammunition for the Italian army.

When the fighting was over, and Italy was united under King Victor Emmanuel, the next step was to elect delegates from the various states to the Chamber of Deputies, Italy's first House of Representatives. Cavour insisted that, if elected, Verdi should sit as a delegate. Verdi considered this absurd, as indeed it was. He was positive that he could do more for freedom through the subtle method of writing an opera than by doodling on a pad during political discussions. But Cavour's arguments, to which were added those of Giuseppe Garibaldi, the red-shirted fighting patriot, persuaded him to make the sacrifice. So strong was his sense of duty, his love of freedom, that he remained a delegate for the full four-year term, although Cavour died shortly after it began.

What has all this to do with *Aïda*? It gives the measure of the man who composed it.

Verdi never stated that any special quality beyond its dramatic intensity attracted him to the story of *Aïda*, but we venture to assume that the "we will overcome" element played its part.

He was in his late fifties, had some twenty-four operas behind him, and was recognized as the leading Italian composer of his time, when the first hint of a commission to write an opera for the Khedive of Egypt was whispered by his friend, Camille du Locle. Du Locle had written the text of *Don Carlo,* which Verdi was rehearsing in Paris at the time. He paid little attention to the preparatory remark by du Locle that a commission in a far distant land might be offered. When a letter did arrive from the Khedive formally inviting Verdi to submit an opera for the festival celebrating the opening of the Suez Canal in November 1869, he was in one of those fallow periods that come to every creative artist when one task has been completed and another not yet begun. He had no libretto awaiting music, nor any story on which to base one. Depressed by the cool reception in Paris of *Don Carlo,* he nursed a grudge against the unappreciative French and against du Locle, who had composed the text. He was nursing his sense of injury, and trying to lose it in the concrete problems of tilling the soil on his estate in Sant' Agata. But both he and his wife, Peppina, were nevertheless on the lookout for a good story. None of those they had considered appealed to him so he wrote to the Khedive that it would be impossible for him to supply an opera in time for the November 1869 event.

Du Locle had a personal interest in finding a story for the Khedive's opera. Whenever he came upon one that had the remotest possibility, he mailed it to Sant' Agata. To save her husband's time and energy, Peppina usually read it first, and if she felt certain that he would reject it, she didn't even show it to him. But one day, a fat envelope arrived which Verdi spied first. He tore it open and glanced through the pages of a long, involved Spanish play by Lopez de Ayala. But from between its pages fluttered four handwritten sheets. They told in brief the story of *Aïda*, by Auguste Mariette Bey. Du Locle was the anonymous sender; he had planned it that way, knowing his Verdi, to add an element of mystery.

Du Locle had sailed up the Nile with Mariette Bey during the preceding winter. Mariette, a Frenchman who had been curator of Egyptian art in the Louvre, had met Verdi in Paris during the production of *Don Carlo*. He had gone to Cairo for a brief visit, had fallen head over heels in love with the country, and remained there to study its people, their customs and their history. So formidable an Egyptologist had he become that the Khedive, Ismail Pasha, had bestowed on him the title of nobility, Bey, and he was known in and out of Egypt as Mariette Bey.

On their river trip, he and du Locle discussed the approaching celebration of the opening of the Suez Canal, and the Khedive's plan to commission an opera. They weighed the merits of Richard Wagner, Charles Gounod, and Giuseppe Verdi, the leading German, French, and Italian composers. Mariette wholeheartedly agreed with du Locle that it had to be Verdi. On the chance, he made a brief outline of *Aïda*, based on an Egyptian story dating back to the time of the Pharaohs. Mariette showed it to the Khedive, and with his approval sent it to Verdi. Verdi then accepted the Khedive's invitation. Wagner would have been eliminated anyway because he was in political hot water at the time, and Gounod had not yet been asked when Verdi accepted. Verdi put du Locle to work at once on a full scenario. At the same time, he wrote the Khedive stating his terms, among these that an Italian poet should write the text. This was hard on du Locle, who had counted on doing so himself, but he bowed out without rancor and remained an interested friend. Verdi's contract with the Khedive gave signal evidence of his business acumen. He demanded a free hand with libretto, conductor, singers, costumes, and scenery, and an honorarium of $30,000 for himself. With the exception of performances in Egypt, all rights were to belong to him. This meant that he collected royalties in all the other places where Aïda was published or performed. In return, the first performance must be in Cairo and nowhere else. The Khedive was to receive one copy of the score for himself, and the opera would be produced in November 1869. This was all the Khedive required. It was a truly munificent contract from Verdi's point of view, signed before a single note of the music was written. But after all, the Suez Canal cost the Khedive over 130 million dollars; compared with this, Verdi's $30,000 fee was a small sum.

Verdi's publishers, Ricordi & Company, were not informed of what was in the wind until after the contract was signed. They had published Verdi when he was young, poor, and unknown, and they had continued to handle his business arrangements. They did not complain of being kept in the dark this time, for the contract was to their advantage as well as Verdi's. They profited from the sale of the score which they published. The publicity attending the spectacular first performance assured Aïda of worldwide attention, with the accompanying bonus of royalties. As performances were more and more in demand, publisher and composer alike were certain to reap a golden harvest. Much of Verdi's share went in generous payments to librettist and performers; later to a hospital for the peasants in the neighboring village of Villanova; later still, to the Casa Verdi, a retirement home in Milan for aged musicians.

Antonio Ghislanzoni was the librettist Verdi chose. He was the editor of the Gazetta Musicale in Milan, a poet, and well known as a composer of opera texts. Besides, he was of a jovial, accommodating disposition and would go along with Verdi as a collaborator, which is what Verdi required. He accepted Verdi's invitation to visit and work with him at Sant' Agata, and Verdi's depression became a thing of the past.

The two men worked well together. Verdi knew exactly the *tinta*—the musical color—that would convey in words his musical thought. And Ghislanzoni, a skillful if not inspired poet, would produce something that could be worked over, changed and polished. When Ghislanzoni went home to complete the libretto, Verdi kept in constant touch by letter. At one point he wrote, "To give you my honest opinion, I don't think this Consecration scene has the importance I was expecting. The characters don't always say what they should say, and the priests aren't priestly enough . . . We want not a cold anthem, but a real scene (Act II, Scene 1) . . . Mariette has said that we can have as many priestesses as we like, so you can add them to the Consecration scene." Many of the lines Verdi himself supplied. The finished work was more Verdian than Ghislanzonian and was later recognized as the best of the sixty librettos credited to Ghislanzoni.

Peppina was happy to see her "man of iron," as she called him (he called himself her old bear), again absorbed in the task of creation. Though the story of *Aïda* is tragic, ending, like Romeo and Juliet, with the lovers expiring together in an underground cavern, laughter leavened the labors of the two men. So well did they collaborate, so cleverly did Peppina ply them with food and wine and black coffee when energy flagged, that the completed libretto sounded as if Italian verse were exactly the right medium for an Egyptian story dating back to the Pharaohs.

As the work progressed, Verdi became an Egyptologist in his own right. He kept in close touch with Mariette Bey, who was to order the scenery and costumes in Paris. He wanted everything to be completely authentic and asked many questions. In the triumphal march of the conquerors, what kind of instruments would Egyptian musicians of that era have played? The answers were to be found in the carvings on the tombs of the Pharaohs. How did the King, the courtiers, the soldiers, the people dress? How did they behave; if there was a tradition, what was it? Were there priestesses as well as priests in the Temple of Isis? What did that powerful Goddess exact of her worshipers? Was it customary to bury traitors alive, to take slaves in battle? He checked Mariette's answers, which came by balloon. He went to libraries and museums, leaving no hieroglyph unturned if it promised to enrich the story and to ensure historical accuracy.

The libretto completed and the research done, Verdi quickly composed the all-important music. It took him only four months. Then he learned that the new Italian opera house in Cairo would not be ready for the opening in 1869 and the opera could not be given until January 1, 1870. However, Mariette wrote that he was about to go to Paris to arrange to have costumes and scenery shipped to Cairo. Verdi waited for further news, but no letter postmarked Paris arrived. No balloon post or any other mail from Paris was being delivered. The War of 1870 between Prussia and France had erupted, the Prussians were besieging Paris, and neither Mariette's letters, he himself, nor the shipments for Cairo could leave the city. The opera, already postponed, had to be set ahead once more. Verdi made some improvements in the score while waiting, but Mariette, costumes, scenery, and the composer remained in cold storage. It was a long chilly winter for all of them. At last the Prussians lifted the siege of Paris in January 1871. At the end of that year, on Christmas Eve, the curtain rose in Cairo on the world premiere of Aïda.

No million-dollar Hollywood spectacular has ever exceeded

that first performance. Musicians, dignitaries, and delegates from all over the world converged on Cairo. So too did friends of Ferdinand de Lesseps, the engineer of the Suez Canal. The Canal had formally been dedicated months before the hieratic opera celebrated its opening, but the thrill was none the less for the delay. The Suez Canal was not then the bone of contention it became a century later. The eyes of the world were fixed no less on the opera than on the titanic engineering feat which created a trade route between the Mediterranean and the Gulf of Suez—a gateway between East and West. Furthermore, the performance took place in a huge opera house especially built for the occasion, notably modernized in having footlights of gas instead of candles. Electric light bulbs, patented by Thomas Edison in 1878, were still in the future. The gaslights could be raised or lowered, without puffing and blowing as with candles. The triumphal pageant could be brightly illuminated, the moonlit love scene appropriately dimmed to create credible moonlight. The stage was large enough to accommodate live elephants in the parade honoring Radames as the conquering hero. They could not be trained to trumpet his success, like the replicas of ancient Egyptian instruments blown by the special brass band in the march, but they could parade on stage with dignity, bearing the victorious Radames' captains on elephant back. The scene was a sensation, and has been so ever since.

The Khedive and his court looked down from their royal box on a glittering assemblage of potentates, musicians, millionaires, journalists from near and far. Filippi, an Italian critic of the day, described the scene. "The Arabians, even the rich, do not love our Italian shows; they prefer the mewlings of their tunes, the monotonous beating of their drums, to all the melodies of the past, present, and future. It is a true miracle to see a turban in a theater of Cairo. Sunday evening, the opera house was crowded before the curtain rose. Many of the boxes were filled with women who neither chattered nor rustled their robes. There was beauty, and there was intelligence, especially among the Greeks and the strangers of rank who abound in Cairo. For truth's sake, I must add that by the side of the most beautiful and the most richly dressed were Coptic and Jewish faces, with strange headdresses, impossible costumes—a howling of colors—no one could deliberately have invented worse. The women of the harem could not be seen. They were in the first three boxes on the right, in the second gallery. Thick white muslin hid their faces from prying glances." It was the custom of the country to keep harem wives in strict seclusion. Women's Liberation, like electricity, was still in the future.

And what of the performance? It would have satisfied even the exacting Verdi. Having declined to conduct it himself, he had shopped around for the next best man. His first choice was Emanuele Muzio, an admiring disciple whom he affectionately called "the little Redhead." Muzio, a shoemaker's son from Busseto, had come to Milan at the age of twenty-three to study with Verdi and had become a son, a Man Friday, an ever-ready assistant. Muzio would have mounted the podium in Cairo with pleasure, but after years of uncertainty, he now had a permanent engagement at the Théâtre des Italiens in Paris. Even the imperious Verdi would not suggest that he sacrifice his job for Aïda.

Angelo Mariani, another old faithful, was also out of the running. He was jealous of Verdi because he feared that his girl friend, Teresa Stolz, the prima donna who was to sing Aïda in Milan, preferred Verdi's ardor to his own. Besides, Verdi was angry with Mariani for deliberately conducting Wagner's Lohengrin in Bologna at the very time when odious comparisons were being made between the two composers. Verdi considered this an unfriendly act by Mariani—as indeed it was. He did not invite him to conduct in Cairo.

The choice finally fell on Giovanni Bottesini, Verdi's friend, the finest double bass player in Europe and, moreover, a highly respected conductor. The opera was in good hands. The singers' names were Italian, the new opera house was Italian, and the seed of Italian opera planted by Verdi in Egypt throve mightily.

Verdi did not go to Cairo for the performance. He pleaded that he was too old—at fifty-seven, he was afraid of seasickness, which had laid him low on a trip to London. The truth was that he was more interested in making a hit with *Aïda* at the Teatro alla Scala in Milan, his home town, than in faraway Egypt. The performance there had long been scheduled, and further delay in Cairo would have jeopardized the Milan production on which he had been working for months. For this, he had engaged Teresa Stolz as Aïda, and invited her to Sant' Agata to work with him on her role. She spent three weeks there being coached. This created two problems. Teresa's lover, Mariani, as already noted, was jealous and resentful. Peppina, Verdi's wife, was equally jealous and looked with disfavor on the long sessions behind closed doors. Having lived with Verdi for twelve years before their marriage, she was not the completely trusting wife. But she set a seal on her lips and tried to persuade herself that her husband's interest was more musical than personal. This took some doing, but in the end she and Teresa became friends. An ex-singer herself, Peppina could make allowances for artistic ambition both in her husband and in the young and beautiful Teresa who was willing to work so hard for Verdi. The other singers, hardly less dedicated, rehearsed all day, every day, sometimes at night, in the Verdis' hotel in Milan or at Sant' Agata. Verdi spared neither himself nor them. Franco Faccio, the young conductor who led the orchestra in Milan, was an adoring disciple who obeyed Verdi's slightest wish. When a question of interpretation arose during rehearsals, Verdi thundered, "You will do as I say because I am Verdi!" It brought results, for the performance at La Scala eclipsed Cairo's in grandeur. An orchestra of ninety, a military band in addition to the orchestra, a chorus of 120, and a herd of elephants created a stunning effect. The evening of February 8, 1872, became legendary in Milan. Verdi was called to the stage again and again—thirty-two curtain calls—was presented with an ivory and gold baton with *Aïda* spelled in rubies on the stem, the name "Verdi," in other precious stones, intertwined, and a diamond star at the tip. In all his years, he had never basked in such a glow of success.

"It is as certain as anything in art history can be that *Aïda* revolutionized modern Italian opera." So wrote W. J. Henderson, a highly respected critic at the turn of the century. And Ernst Reyer, a French critic who was a Wagner enthusiast, commented immediately after the Cairo performance on Verdi's use of "all the artifices of fugue and counterpoint, new harmonies, more important accompaniment to new forms of melody."

No wonder then that *Aïda* became a cherished item in the repertoire of every opera house worthy of the name.

Every town in Italy wanted to hear *Aïda*, whether or not its opera house could provide stalls for the elephants. Verdi could have his choice. He elected to go first to Naples, then to Parma. In Naples, the impact of the opera was much the same as in Milan. The past opposition to *Un Ballo in maschera* was forgotten, for La Bomba was no longer King; Naples had been taken into the fold of King Victor Emmanuel. After the performance a torchlight procession, led by trumpeters blowing the March from *Aïda* on reproductions of ancient Egyptian instruments* followed Verdi to his hotel. They clamored, "Speech, speech," until he came out on the balcony to show himself to his admirers. But when the Verdis returned to Sant' Agata all was not peaches and cream. Dozens of letters awaited them;

* "Six straight trumpets of the old Egyptian kind, which are no longer in use, and therefore had to be specially made" wrote Verdi.

most were fan mail praising *Aïda*, but there were some which accused him of imitating Wagner, then the idol of Germany. Verdi had walked out on *Lohengrin*, did not admire the much vaunted heroic orchestra, and the taxing arias and recitatives that Wagner wished on his singers. He had no idea of imitating Wagner—quite the contrary—and snorted angrily when he was accused of doing so.

Not until 1876 was Paris, the acknowledged leader in "modern" music of the time, permitted by Verdi to present *Aïda*, and then he deliberately stipulated the Théâtre des Italiens in preference to the splendiferous Grand Opéra, which had twice done him wrong. He still nursed a grudge against it, for he had stalked out of the rehearsals of his *Sicilian Vespers* twenty years earlier after a disagreement with the stage director, swearing never to return. And when he did return for a production of his *Don Carlo* he was again so dissatisfied with the treatment he received that he had no desire to face the French public a third time. His excellent memory did not fail him in total recall of displeasure. It was four years after *Aïda* triumphed in the Théâtre des Italiens in Paris that Verdi graciously allowed it to be performed at the Grand Opéra. The President of France then made handsome amends for past misunderstandings. He gave Verdi an official banquet and made him an officer of the Legion of Honor, an order of merit generally bestowed on military heroes or civil servants.

To the composer belong most of the spoils, but it is only fair to mention some of the many distinguished singers who have brought *Aïda*'s characters to life since the historic first performance in Cairo. Pozzini, Grossi, Mongini, Stella, Medini, Costa, Bottardi, famous in their day, are today names only. Those who sang at La Scala, closely identified with Verdi himself, are more familiar, especially Teresa Stolz and Maria Waldmann, who later sang in his *Manzoni Requiem*. Fancelli, Pandolfini, Maini were hero, King, and High Priest. In more recent times there have been Zinka Milanov, Maria Callas, Renata Tebaldi, Leontyne Price, Birgit Nilsson, and Martina Arroyo in the title role; Mario del Monaco, Carlo Bergonzi, Franco Corelli, and Richard Tucker as Radames; and Ebe Stignani, Giulietta Simionato, Fedora Barbieri, and Grace Bumbry as Amneris. And still they come, and will continue to come. To appear in this opera is many a singer's dream.

To the credit of the United States, *Aïda* was staged in New York only two years after the Cairo production, even before it became popular in Europe. Max Strakosch, an enterprising impresario who had moved from Vienna to the United States, put on a magnificent performance at the Academy of Music on November 26, 1873.

To talk about an opera is one thing, actually to see and hear it is another. There is a step between that should not be overlooked. The music of *Aïda* fires with enthusiasm the nonprofessional as well as the opera buff, but the fire burns brighter for those who familiarize themselves with the score before attending their first performance.

To follow one of the magnificent recordings with a libretto or a vocal score, noting particularly the outstanding arias and their place in the story, is enjoyable homework, worth doing. Of the recordings listed below, complete versions of the opera are to be preferred, for with *Aïda* the whole is greater than—rather than equal to—the sum of all its parts. The indefinable *plus* of *Aïda* raises it above the usual run of grand opera. A jazzed-up version entitled *My Darlin' Aïda* was produced in New York in the fall of 1952. However fleeting its success, its title struck home. This opera is, was, and ever will be *My Darlin' Aïda* to the opera world.

RECORDINGS*

Nilsson, Bumbry, Corelli, Mehta, Rome Op.   3-Angel S-3716
Excerpts from above   Angel S-36566;
        8XS-36566 (cartridge tape); 4XS-36566 (cassette tape)
Price, Bumbry, Domingo, Milnes, Raimondi, Leinsdorf, London
    Sym., Alldis Cho.   3-RCA LSC-6198
Excerpts from above   RCA LSC-3275;
        R8S-1237 (cartridge tape); RK-1237 (cassette tape)
Price, Gorr, Tozzi, Merrill, Vickers, Solti, Rome Op.
                    3-London 1393; D31164 (cassette tape)
Tebaldi, Simionato, Bergonzi, MacNeil, Karajan   3-London 1313
Excerpts from above   London 25206;
        M69025 (cartridge tape); M31025 (cassette tape)
Nilsson, Hoffman, Ottolini, Quilico, Pritchard, Royal Op.
    (selections)   London 25798

Callas, Tucker, Gobbi, Serafin   3-Angel 3525
Caniglia, Stignani, Gigli, Bechi, Serafin, Rome Op.
                                                 3-Seraphim 6016
Curtis-Verna, Corelli, Questa   3-Everest/Cetra S-401/3E
Excerpts from above   Pickwick S-407E; Everest/Cetra 7401E;
                                    CEV-2401 (cassette tape)
Milanov, Barbieri, Björling, Warren, Christoff, Perlea, Rome Op.
                                            3-RCA Victrola 6119
Nelli, Gustavson, Tucker, Valdengo, Toscanini, NBC Sym., Cho.
                                          3-RCA Victrola S-6113E
Tebaldi, Stignani, Del Monaco, Protti, Erede   3-Richmond 63002
Excerpts from above   Richmond 23037
Gadski, Caruso, Homer, Amato (selections)   RCA Victrola 1623

* Taken from Schwann-1 Record & Tape Guide, February 1973, and
from Schwann-2 Record & Tape Guide, Spring 1973.

Mussorgsky's
BORIS GODUNOV

MUSSORGSKY'S

Boris Godunov

A stark, rugged, tumultuous masterpiece, full of paradoxes and contradictions; a tremendous, awe-inspiring compendium of the soul of the Russian people; a monument of much that is most typical in Russian musical drama, and at the same time a personal, inimitable work; music of such transcendent greatness that it is hard to speak of it without raving—these are the terms which have been applied to *Boris Godunov*. "I vividly remember living *Boris,* and in my brain, the time I lived *Boris* has left precious, indestructible landmarks," said Mussorgsky. The landmarks may have been indestructible, but the composer was not. Seven years after the first performance of this masterpiece, he died, penniless, at the age of forty-two, an incurable alcoholic, bloated, bearded, and besotted, but beloved.

Luck played an important part in the creation of *Boris Godunov.* It is one of the iffiest of operas. If one thing hadn't come into Mussorgsky's life just when it did, then another could not have followed, and this opera would never have come into being. Certainly, the artistic climate at the court of Tsar Alexander II was anything but favorable to music and musicians. Painters were given commissions and the title "artist of the state" for executing them. Writers too were recognized as artists, but musicians were regarded as second-class citizens. They could

not well be anything else, for until Anton Rubinstein founded
the St. Petersburg Conservatory in 1862, and his brother Nikolai the Moscow Conversatory a few years later, there were no
conservatories in all Russia where professional training could be
had. This does not mean that there was no music. Amateurs
flourished in the upper classes—self-taught, privately taught, or
taught by travel in Europe. Folk songs and dances, handed down
from one generation to the next, resounded from the cottages
where the peasants lived, the fields where they worked, the
nurseries where they tended their masters' children. If Mussorgsky's nurse had not steeped him in this lore, if he had instead sat docilely at the feet of the conservatory professors, to be
molded in their image, Boris might have come out differently.
Again, if he had not, at the impressionable age of eighteen, met
Mily Balakirev, a natural-born musician who became his mentor, and the circle of young musicians, artists, and writers who
gathered around Balakirev, his genius might have been nipped
in the bud for lack of nourishment.

A final and considerable if. If, at about the same time he met
Balakirev, he had not heard Glinka's opera A Life for the Tsar,
which moved him to the very depths of his soul, he might never
have developed the fierce nationalism he displayed in Boris,
indelibly stamped "Made in Russia."

Mikhail Glinka was the first nationalist composer in Russia.
His life (1804–1857) overlapped Mussorgsky's (1839–1881).
His sister, Ludmila Shestakova, became Mussorgsky's close
friend. Glinka was described by another composer, Peter Ilich
Tchaikovsky, as "a dilettante who played now on the violin, now
on the piano, who composed colorless quadrilles and fantasies on
stylish themes, who tried his hand at serious forms such as quar-
tets and quintets and songs, but who composed nothing but
banalities in the taste of the 1830s until—!!! Suddenly, in the

thirty-fourth year of his life, he produces an opera which, by its genius, breadth, originality, and flawless technique stands on a level with the greatest and most profound music." This opera was *A Life for the Tsar*, highly approved by the Tsar and his court, as indeed why not? Whatever the merits of the music, the story was bound to appeal. It glorified a Russian peasant, Ivan Susanin, who deliberately led a battalion of the attacking Polish army away from the monastery where the newly crowned young Tsar was being held in safe-keeping. By so doing, Susanin saved the Tsar's life at the sacrifice of his own. It took Glinka four acts and an epilogue, and a lot of music, some of it literally quoted folk songs, to tell this story. His opera was a "first" in several respects—the first to choose an all-Russian subject, the first to contain built-in Russian folk song, the first to elevate a peasant to a hero. It struck a responsive chord in every Russian breast. To Mussorgsky, already deeply in sympathy with the peasantry, it was a beacon, guiding him to the passionate proclamation in music of Russian identity. *Boris Godunov* emulated *A Life for the Tsar* in its nationalism only. Its language is Mussorgsky's own, poignant, personal, unforgettable.

In his life, Mussorgsky did resemble Glinka. Both were sons of wealthy landowners, both were elegant amateurs in their youth. Both evinced the same sharp cleavage between their youth and their artistic maturity. Mussorgsky was born into the middle class—neither upper nor lower—of Russian society. His father inherited broad lands from a grandfather who had unconventionally married a serf's daughter. Modest Mussorgsky liked to boast of the nonblue blood in his veins. His mother, whom he adored, was a romantic lady who wrote sentimental poetry and played the piano quite well. Modest was one of four sons, two of whom died in early childhood.

As to his musical education, the remark of a concert pianist a century later is applicable: "We all seem to be geniuses, and we all are taught by our mothers." Modest's mother initiated him so successfully into the mysteries of the keyboard, that at seven he was able to play some pieces by Franz Liszt, and at eleven he entertained a big party of his parents' friends at the piano. He was a happy child. The family estate where he roamed at will comprised many acres of woodland and stream, and many serfs tilled its fields. The manor house stood on a hill overlooking a lake, where he fished and swam. His peasant nurse told the small boy tales of ancient Russia, sang him its folk songs and religious chants. With every breath he drew, he breathed in the savor of his native land—its mysticism, its spacious grandeur, its steppes and valleys, its traditions.

His mother's piano instruction was supplemented by private lessons from a teacher in nearby St. Petersburg, until he entered the School for Cadets of the Guards. He was thirteen. Although his father was sufficiently interested in his musical talent to pay for piano lessons, it doesn't seem to have occurred to him that a military school was not the best place for a sensitive, artistic boy. All wealthy young men became officers in the army as a matter of course, so both Modest and his brother Filaret were automatically enrolled in the School for Cadets. For Modest this was particularly unwise. He kept up his music in a desultory way, as a social accomplishment, but he learned little that was good and much that was bad for him. The head of the school discouraged reading as unbecoming to an officer and a gentleman, and actually reproved Modest when he found him absorbed in a book. Wine, women, and song had priority over other occupations. He encouraged the students to drink aristocratic champagne in preference to proletarian vodka and didn't care how much they drank, so long as they didn't reel back to school on foot or in a public conveyance but in a discreet private carriage. When, at seventeen, Modest graduated into the snobbish Probajensky regiment, he was thoroughly prepared for the extravagant life of its officers, which consisted of gambling, dancing, making love, and drinking. Of the four, drinking appealed to him most. He was described at this period as "a very callow, most elegant, perfectly contrived little officer: brand-new close-fitting uniform, toes well turned out, hair well oiled and carefully smoothed, hands shapely and well cared for." A far cry indeed from the bearded, bloated Mussorgsky as portrayed on his deathbed by the painter Repin. Yet the man with the ravaged visage in the painting is what the dapper dandy of the Probajensky regiment became. Here enters another if. If his father had not exposed his gifted son to this type of career, might Modest have become the Russian Beethoven, with numerous epic works to his credit? Who knows? Instead, he wrecked his health and acquired one of the worst of bad habits, drinking to excess. When he resigned from the army, at eighteen, he suffered an agonizing nervous breakdown, from which it took months to recover.

All was not lost, however. While he was still in the regiment, a brother officer introduced him to the composer Alexander Dargomyzhsky, whose opera *Russalka* was then in the limelight. Artists, writers, critics, musicians gathered in his home. It was here that Modest met Mily Balakirev. The critic Vladimir Stasov, the composers Alexander Borodin, Nikolai Rimsky-Korsakov, and César Cui came at various times. The three last, with Mussorgsky and Balakirev, became "the Five" of Russian music. They met often, to analyze the works not only of their compatriots, Glinka and Dargomyzhsky, but of Hector Berlioz, Franz Liszt, and Robert Schumann, the romantic "moderns" of the nineteenth century. This was "cabman's music,"

that is, music considered nonacceptable by the conservatory professors and aristocratic conservatives—for example Tchaikovsky.
These meetings then and during the 1860s were the most precious hours in Modest's life. They gave impetus to his determination to quit the military for music. Lonely for music and its
practitioners, he clung to Balakirev, his "dear Mily," his teacher,
friend, counselor, and confidant. He wrote him long letters,
studied Ludwig van Beethoven's symphonies with him, and composed songs and piano sonatas as homework. Time went on.
His style became increasingly daring and original. Gradually he
drifted away from his teacher, who at one point denounced him
as "a thorough idiot." He strained too hard at the leash, refused
to submit forever to his teacher's dictatorship. He was the first
to break away; as Balakirev became more set in his ways, the
other disciples followed Mussorgsky's example.

Modest's easy life changed drastically when, on February 3,
1861, Tsar Alexander II issued a proclamation that freed the
serfs. Traditionally, since the days of Tsar Boris Godunov, they
had been bound to serve the master who owned the land they
occupied, to remain with him and render the fruits of their
labor whether he treated them well or badly. Now they could
pick and choose and move about at will, a mild form of free
enterprise. Although there is no record of dissatisfaction among
the serfs on Karevo, the Mussorgsky estate, the edict created a
profound upheaval. "Let my people go" was Modest's con-
clusion after trying for a year to devise some way to carry on.
The estate was liquidated, and he took a civil service job in
the Department of Communications. He was twenty-two.

During the six years between this unexpected turn of events
and the beginning of *Boris,* Modest nurtured his body meagerly
on his small government salary, enriched his spirit and matured
his mind with the encouragement of a growing circle of friends.

For a time, he lived in a sort of commune of young men, with whom he held nightly discussions of new ideas and ideals that inflamed his imagination. Then, besides Dargomyzhsky and the Five, there were Alexandra Purgold, a singer, and her sister Nadezhda, a pianist so accomplished that Modest nicknamed her "little orchestra." The whole circle had nicknames—Modest was Musoryanin or Modinka, or anything they chose to call him. Ludmila Shestakova, Glinka's sister, kept open house for musicians, and Modest was a special favorite. Vladimir Stasov, the critic, was to become his guardian angel in the dark days when he staggered, drunk and discouraged, from one cheap café to another. Vladimir's brother Dmitri too, a musician, was always close by. And Vladimir Nikolsky, a professor of literature at the University of St. Petersburg, specialized in the study of Alexander Pushkin, the Russian Shakespeare. It was Nikolsky who called Modest's attention to Pushkin's play *Boris Godunov,* he who looked over Modest's shoulder at the script and suggested some revisions. All of these friends aided and abetted Modest in the realization of his opera. And they seconded him in the beliefs he developed.

He believed in realism, in protraying people and events not prettied up but as they really are. Truth before beauty was his motto. He believed in nationalism, in writing music that couldn't be mistaken for anything but Russian. In *Boris,* he quoted native folk songs, not literally, but in such a way as to convey the unmistakable flavor of the Russian people, like a clove of garlic in a salad dressing. He believed in spontaneity, and delighted in improvising songs at the piano, to be used later, perhaps, in a song cycle or an opera. If they were funny or entertaining, so much the better. One of the nicknames Nadezhda gave him, in fact, was Humor. His letters and music (for example, *The Song of the Flea*) evince good reason for the name. Nadezhda complained that, though humorous, he lacked warmth and tenderness and was a terrific egotist. But this was because he didn't propose marriage to her sister Alexandra; in fact, he remained a bachelor. He was from the start against the Establishment, the conservatory professors hired by the two Rubinsteins, the German-dictated study of form and theory, even the *Leitmotifs* of Wagner. Inspiration from within and from works he honestly admired guided him.

Of "the Five," Modest was by far the most daring and different, the first to write according to the beliefs they all averred, and which he set forth in letters and conversations with them. "I want to say that if the expression in sound of human thought and feeling is truly produced by me in music, and this representation is musical and artistic, then the thing is in the bag." He aimed "to tug at the heartstrings," "to catch the intonations of the human voice in music." "What I project is the melody of life, not of classicism." Of the Russian people he said, "When I sleep, I see them, when I eat, I think of them, when I drink, I can visualize them, huge, unpainted, without tinsel, with integrity." He expressed the wish, in his music, "to embrace Mother Russia in all her simple-souled girth." A critic, hearing *Boris* for the first time, exclaimed, "Yes, this is real Russian history."

How real is it, historically? It is true that both Pushkin and Mussorgsky looked up the story of the Tsar Boris Feodorovich in Karamzin's *History of the Holy Roman Empire*. But they learned from it that the real Boris, who reigned from 1598 to 1605, was a benevolent despot as tsars go. Brother-in-law of the weak Tsar Feodor, whose prime minister he was, he was drafted into becoming the Tsar against his will. Far from murdering and conspiring for the rulership, he did his best to dodge it. He was not even suspected of killing the boy Dmitri, Feodor's son, who stood between him and the throne. According to the prevailing rules, he was reasonably just and merciful, except for one big blot on his scutcheon. It was he who decreed that serfs must remain on the land where they were born and serve its masters, thus condemning them to virtual slavery. He did this to curry favor with the boyars, the nobles who represented the Russian "military-industrial" complex of the time. He desperately needed the boyars to wage wars, and to keep the people down. Naturally the serfs hated him for this law, which remained in effect until Mussorgsky's day, almost three centuries. The Pushkin-Mussorgsky story differs somewhat, either because they interpreted Boris' character in their own way, or because they took artistic liberties with the truth to make the tale more dramatic, even gruesome. In the opera, he is seen as a man tortured by a guilty conscience, a man who has ascended the throne over the dead body of a murdered child. He is finally driven mad, and dies in a frenzy of fear and remorse. The text, half prose, half poetry, half in recitative, half sung, was written by Mussorgsky himself.

THE CAST

Boris Godunov, the Tsar	*Bass*
Feodor, his son	*Mezzo-soprano*
Xenia, his daughter	*Soprano*
Nurse	*Mezzo-soprano*
Tchelkalov, clerk of the Duma	*Baritone or bass*
Pimen, an old monk	*Bass*
Grigori, a young monk, later known as Dmitri	*Tenor*
Prince Shuiski, Boris' adviser	*Tenor*
Marina, a Polish girl, daughter of the Governor of Sandomir	*Mezzo-soprano*
Hostess of the Inn	*Mezzo-soprano*

Varlaam ⎫		*Bass*
Missail ⎭ vagabond monks		*Tenor*
Rangoni, a Jesuit priest		*Baritone or bass*
Police officer		*Bass*
Simpleton		*Tenor*

Time: 1598–1605
Place: Russia and Poland
First performance in St. Petersburg, January 27, 1874.

PROLOGUE*

This is far too significant a part of the opera to be entitled
a prologue. It is really Act I, for it sets the mood of the opera.
The conflicting groups—the Tsar's brilliant court on the one
hand, the protesting people on the other—are immediately
made visible with dramatic and uncompromising honesty. Yet,
although this is what the opera is about, the Prologue is no
more closely connected with Act I than that with Act II.
Like life itself, *Boris Godunov* is a series of happenings which
chance to affect one man, the Tsar, but which are not themselves related. They are flashed like a movie into sight and
hearing, one after another. Only after the finale of Act IV is
it made clear that Mother Russia herself, her grandeur and
power and wealth, her misery, cruelty, oppression, and crime,
is symbolized. The play is like one of Shakespeare's historical

* The text of *Boris* has been translated from Russian into French,
German, Italian, English, and other languages. Since I am unfamiliar
with Russian, I have not given first lines in the original language,
but in English, hoping that those who listen to performances, recordings,
or broadcasts will be helped to recognize them because of their place in
the detailed story.

dramas, with Imperial Russia as the heroine, her life woven from the triple strand of Tsar, People, and Church.

SCENE I

The curtain rises on a stage in semidarkness. Peasants and townsfolk mill around in the courtyard of the Novodievich Monastery near Moscow. The police are clearly in evidence. They are there to make sure that the people pray for the right candidate. Their "little father," Tsar Ivan, has died, and they pray for his soul in heaven. His young son, Dmitri, has also died, and there is no heir to the throne. His prime minister, Boris Godunov, has been the interim ruler. He has been offered the crown but has refused. He is at this moment in the church, being offered the crown for a second time, and the people have been summoned to implore him to accept it. There are dark murmurs that Boris is the murderer of Dmitri, and that he re- fuses because of his guilty conscience. Nevertheless, the people pray—what difference does it make to them who rules? Besides, the police crack their whips and order them to their knees with special vigor when Tchelkalov, the secretary of the Duma, the Russian parliament, comes out of the church to make an announcement. This is the signal for a noisy outburst of en- forced prayer. But Tchelkalov's news is not good. Boris has again refused to take office, and Russia remains leaderless.

A chorus of pilgrims is heard, swelling in volume as the holy men approach. They distribute amulets and go into the church, their song dying gently as they recede. Theirs is a singu- larly beautiful chorus, particularly in contrast with the disjointed phrases of prayer, lament, and supplication that precede it. Ap- parently it is enough to melt the heart of Boris, for the curtain rises on

SCENE 2—*The Coronation Scene*

This is as brilliant as the first was somber. Boris has at last consented, and is at this very moment being crowned in the Cathedral of the Assumption. A rich orchestral march preludes the scene. In the square inside the Kremlin and outside the Cathedral, the people, again on their knees, wait for their newly crowned Tsar to show himself to them. As before, the police are there to cue them in to shout at the right moment. The boyars march in a stately procession across the courtyard. Prince Shuiski, Boris' right hand man, appears on the steps of the Cathedral. "Long life to the Tsar, Tsar Boris Feodorovich!" he sings. The boyars and the kneeling masses echo the cry, church bells join in a joyous rhythmic clangor as Boris comes from the Cathedral. He is clad in gorgeous robes of state, with crown and scepter, but his mood is solemn. He pauses to sing a heartfelt prayer: "My soul is sad. What nameless fear grips my heart with ominous foreboding! Oh, righteous judge, oh, mighty Father! From heaven above, look on my tears with mercy and bestow your blessing upon my reign! And grant that I may be good, just, and merciful as You to my people!" He scatters gold pieces, and while the people scramble for them, he invites them to be his guests at a great feast. All are welcome. First, however, he and they will pray together at the tomb of the dead Tsar in the Cathedral of the Archangel across the square. Despite the brilliance of music, scenery, and costumes, there is deep underlying sadness in this scene. Boris, a man convinced against his will, confesses to forebodings and a sense of insecurity. He is not deceived by the prayers of a populace coerced by the police to express sentiments he knows they do not feel. Besides, he is a guilty man.

ACT I

SCENE 1—*A cell in a monastery, five years later*

A white-bearded, aged monk, Pimen, is writing laboriously under the dim light of an oil lamp. It is dawn. On a pallet nearby, the young monk Grigori lies sleeping. Pimen rejoices aloud, at some length, that he has reached the last page in the chronicle of Russian history to which he has devoted his life. "Still one last tale and my chronicle is ended."

Grigori awakens with a cry, "Again that dream! That self-same dream! That nagging accursed dream!" For the third time, he says, he has had the same nightmare. "I was atop a tower, all Moscow at my feet. The people were like ants below. They pointed at me and laughed. I felt terrified and fell from the tower, and woke up." Pimen calms him. "Your youthful blood surges. Give yourself over to prayer and fasting, and your dreams will be of happy pictures."

Pimen then relates legendary tales of Russia, concluding with a story about the present reigning Tsar, Boris. He tells Grigori that Boris murdered the Tsarevich Dmitri in the very monastery where they are at that moment. "How old would the Tsarevich be if he had lived?" asks Grigori. "Exactly your age," replies Pimen. The young man draws a deep breath and his own conclusions. Perhaps, he muses, the child Tsarevich was not murdered after all, perhaps he himself is Dmitri. That nightmare must mean something. In the twinkling of an eye, he is tranformed in his imagination from the humble monk Grigori to the glittering Tsarevich Dmitri. The bells ring for matins, and Pimen goes to pray, leaving Grigori in a maze of hopes and fears.

SCENE 2—*A tavern on the Lithuanian border of Russia*

The hostess bustles about her taproom, hoping for customers. She sings a gay folk song, one of the few light moments in the opera. She is a lusty, life-loving character, marvelously characterized in the music she sings, though hers is a small part. "Once I caught a duckling with feathers green and blue. Oh thou, my darling drake, Come again, my mate so true." Her song is interrupted by the arrival of Varlaam and Missail, wandering mendicant priests. She feels obliged, though reluctantly, to give food and drink to the holy men. They are soon befuddled. Varlaam's song, *Long ago at Kazan where our troops were fighting,* begins as a legend from the days of Tsar Ivan, and ends as a rowdy drinking song. Grigori, escaped from the monastery and disguised, comes in and orders food and drink. Chatting with the hostess, he learns that the police are on his trail, and gets her to tell him the shortest way to Poland. She warns him to bypass the guardhouse where he will be asked to show his papers, and he notes her instructions carefully. He plans to set himself up in Poland as Dmitri, the supposedly murdered heir to the Russian empire. From now on, he is known as Dmitri.

Two policemen enter with a warrant for his arrest. Neither of them can read the description of the wanted man on the warrant. The false Dmitri obligingly offers to read it for them, and substitutes for the description of himself a description of Varlaam, who, drunk as he is, looks every inch the vagrant. At the threat of arrest, Varlaam insists on seeing the warrant.

Being a monk, he too can read. He reads the correct description aloud. Dmitri escapes through the window.

ACT II

The pleasant domestic setting of this act, the nursery in Boris' apartments in the Kremlin, is deceptive, for tragedy immediately intrudes. Boris' sixteen-year-old daughter Xenia sits weeping over the death of her fiancé, singing "Where art thou, my betrothed? Where art thou, my loved one?" The old nurse tries to comfort her, and sings "The Song of the Gnat," the kind of folksy children's song that Mussorgsky did so well in *The Nursery*. Xenia's little brother, the Tsarevich Feodor, chides the nurse for choosing such a melancholy tune, and she invites him to do better if he can. He responds with the "Clapping Game Song." "Here's a tale about this and that, How a hen gave birth to a calf, And a piglet laid an egg." The nurse joins him in clapping on the first beat of each measure, and Xenia permits herself a watery smile. Boris enters, and the merriment freezes into breathlessness. But he tenderly bids Xenia dry her tears, and go with the nurse to find playmates who will distract her. Obediently, they leave, and he is alone with his small son. Together, they pore over the map of Russia, and Boris impresses on Feodor the greatness of the country he will one day, perhaps soon, have to govern. Boris' heart is heavy. Sinking into a chair, he sings the notable recitative aria: "I have attained to power. Six years have passed since first I ruled over Russia, but still no peace returns to my remorseful soul." He mourns that God is punishing him for the murder of the Tsarevich Dmitri by taking the life of his future son-

in-law; that all Russia groans in misery and the people blame
their misfortunes on him; that his nobles plot against him and
in Poland revolution is rife. He cannot sleep at night, haunted
by visions of the murdered Dmitri. As he approaches the end
of the aria, a noise is heard offstage. A boyar comes to ask an
audience for Prince Shuiski. At the same time, little Feodor
runs in to explain to his father that the noise was caused by
the nurses, who were attacked by a pet parakeet. He climbs on
Boris' lap and tells so wittily of the commotion caused by the
bird that his father for a moment casts off his somber mood.
Not for long, however. Prince Shuiski is ushered in, and little
Feodor is banished from the room. The prince brings dire news.
A pretender (Dmitri) has arisen in Poland and is being ac-
claimed by many as the true ruler. The Pope himself has recognized his claim. If he succeeds in crossing the border into
Russia, the disaffected people may decide to join him. What is
to be done? Boris bursts into a tirade against Shuiski, whom he
accuses, with reason, of treachery. He orders the border closed
and guarded, and asks the Pretender's name. "Dmitri," replies Shuiski. Boris frantically demands Shuiski's assurance that
Dmitri is dead and buried. Shuiski cunningly plays on his
fears, telling him that the boy Dmitri's body lay with others
for five days after the murder on the steps of the monastery,
but that while the other bodies decomposed, the Tsarevich's
flesh remained pink and healthy, as though he were alive.
"Enough," cries Boris, choking. He signals that he wishes to
be left alone, and sinks back into his chair. "Oh, I am choking!
Give me air! I feel all my blood rushing to my head. I am
sinking!" He believes that he is dying, and in his anguish he
sees the ghost of little Dmitri. Terrified, he bids it begone. The
chiming of the clock drives him to further madness; it must be
his death knell! Shuiski meanwhile has remained hidden,

where he could see and hear Boris' ravings. Unobserved, he leaves, and the scene ends with a half-mad Boris, alone, praying distractedly for God's mercy on his guilty soul.

ACT III

SCENE 1—*Marina's room in the Castle of Mnichek*

The rich and ambitious Polish girl Marina Mnichek, daughter of the Governor of Sandomir, sits at her dressing table, being dressed and bejeweled for a ball, while her serving women sing a flattering chorus. Obviously, this scene has no connection with anything that preceded it. The composer boldly inserted it after his first version had been rejected because it contained no love interest. Listeners to the opera might well exclaim, "This is so sudden!" But Marina, young and beautiful and with an eye on Dmitri, supplies the required touch of romance. However, it is a cruel, cold romance. She dismisses her maids—"Enough! Your lovely lady thanks you"—and, alone, sings a magnificent aria that reveals her character as it really is. She bewails the emptiness of her life, her boredom with the suitors who pursue her, and goes on to declare, with superb detachment, that she will win the pretender, Dmitri, for her own, and at his side will rule over Russia. At the thought that the hated Russians will grovel at her feet, she laughs aloud, and the aria ends on that laugh.

At this moment, enter Rangoni, a Jesuit priest. He is her spiritual adviser, and she is duty bound to obey him. He too is ambitious, and wily besides. He encourages Marina to ensnare Dmitri, and promises his assistance. He tells her that she must pledge herself to carry the tenets of the Roman Catholic

Church to Russia on her rise to power. Only if she does so will he consent to the marriage. She demurs. The sainthood he promises as her reward interests her far less than more worldly pleasures. But he threatens her with hell-fire until, terrified, she falls to her knees and promises to obey. The curtain falls.

This is the scene about which Mussorgsky wrote elatedly, "I am finishing the scene, the Jesuit has given me no rest for two nights in a row. That's fine, I love it."

SCENE 2—*A garden in the Castle of Mnichek*

Dmitri enters, mooning over a love letter from Marina bidding him meet her at the fountain in her garden at this witching hour. Here he is, and while waiting in the moonlight he pours out his love in a tenor aria. "At midnight, in the garden at the fountain. O divine voice! With what rapture you fill my heart!" He dares to hope that his love is reciprocated. But into the moonlight steps not Marina but the priest Rangoni. He works on the emotional young man, telling him in all secrecy that Marina pines for him, that gossip has reared its ugly head to impugn her virtue, that Dmitri must marry her to save her reputation. "Only take me to her and let me speak my love, and I will pay you any price," he cries impetuously. Well pleased, Rangoni extorts a promise that he, and he alone, will be Dmitri's spiritual adviser when he ascends the throne of Russia. He asks that he may follow Dmitri at all times, may watch over his comings and goings and know his thoughts, may guard and keep him like a son. "Yes," cries the impetuous Dmitri, "you shall remain with me always if you will bring me to Marina." Their duet ends as guests at the banquet pour out into the garden. Rangoni melts away into the darkness, and Dmitri hastily conceals himself in the shrubbery.

The "Polacca," danced by the guests, brings in Marina on the arm of an elderly nobleman, who talks of his love for her, while the nobles softly conspire against Russia. Cool, bored, Marina promises nothing. All re-enter the castle, and Dmitri voices his jealous rage at seeing her with another man. He is dry tinder, ready for a spark, which she strikes when she returns, alone, exclaiming, "Dmitri! Tsarevich!"

"You are here, my dove, my beautiful one. How dreary, how long the moments of waiting!" he replies.

There is a long, wonderful duet in which she plays cruelly on his passion. When he expresses scruples about leading a rebellion, she taunts him with being a weakling. He is stung. They argue back and forth. Finally, he swears that he will ride into Russia and annihilate Boris, with her beside him. At once she is all tenderness and loving kindness. The mood of the music in their duet varies with the argument—Alla mazurka, Andante amoroso, Recitative, Adagio, Agitato. Even in translation the feeling of the words and the personalities of the couple who sing them are extraordinarily expressed in the music.

As Dmitri and Marina fall into each other's arms, Rangoni reappears. He rubs his hands with satisfaction, and comments that he is content, for it is in truth not Marina but the Church that has won the day.

ACT IV

SCENE 1—*A hall in the Kremlin*

A heavily pulsing prelude is played by the orchestra as the boyars take their seats on benches facing the Tsar's throne, which stands empty. They discuss the mounting rebellion, and pronounce that it must be halted at all costs and the pretender killed without mercy. Prince Shuiski comes late to the meeting. He describes Boris' distraught state as he had witnessed it. While he speaks, Boris himself staggers in. He is still raving, still bidding the murdered Tsarevich's ghost begone.

"Away, away! Who says Murder? I am not a murderer. He lives! The child lives! And Shuiski, the lying perjurer, shall be quartered!"

Shuiski speaks to Boris soothingly and he pulls himself together. He calls upon the boyars to pledge loyalty to him and to stamp out the traitors. Shuiski then asks if he will give audience to an aged priest who has come to comfort him. Seated on his throne, with its diamond-studded arms, he is still an imposing though ravaged figure. Pimen is brought before him. He bids him speak. Pimen's tale does not have the desired effect, though the music flows gently. An aged shepherd, blind since birth, says Pimen, heard in a dream the voice of the boy, Tsarevich Dmitri, bidding him pray beside his grave. The shepherd obeyed. Wonder of wonders, his eyesight was restored. A miracle! At this, Boris utters a cry and falls unconscious. The boyars rush to him. Feebly he asks for his son, and Feodor is brought to him. He requests that they be left alone together, and a touching scene ensues. "Farewell, my son, I am dying . . . soon you will reign . . . Do not seek to know by what path I gained the throne . . . You do not need to know. You are the legitimate ruler." He gives the boy last instructions on how to rule, and prays for mercy for his tortured, guilty soul. The boyars return, priests sing prayers for his departing soul, church bells toll in farewell. Boris starts up, shouting, "I am still your Tsar!" but adds weakly, pointing to Feodor, "Forgive me. There, there is your Tsar," and falls back, lifeless, in his chair.

This impressive scene provides a dramatic climax, and in the original, as Act IV, Scene 2, it marked the end of the opera. Historically, Boris died before Dmitri seized the throne and murdered Feodor and his mother, taking Boris' daughter Xenia for his mistress. Historically, Dmitri was a cruel, unjust Tsar, and was overthrown after two years. It served him right! None of this is revealed in the opera, however.

When Mussorgsky revised *Boris*, he reversed Scene 1 and Scene 2, and it is now performed sometimes one way, sometimes another, at the discretion of the conductor. Both scenes are equally moving, it all depends upon where the emphasis is placed. In one, the guilty yet pitiable Tsar holds our interest, in the other, the People, crude and cruel, yet with a kind of appealing innocence.

SCENE 2—*A clearing in the forest near the Russian village of Kromy, whose walls loom in the distance*

A crowd of peasants and townspeople rushes in, manhandling a boyar whom they have seized. They mock and taunt him at some length, until a group of urchins, teasing the town simpleton, join the game. The boys steal the simpleton's few pennies, but as he cries aloud, they are in turn interrupted by Varlaam and Missail, the vagabond priests last seen in the inn in Act I. They speak, whipping up the people's fury at the poverty and hunger, the unjust punishments and sufferings they have had to endure under Boris. They urge them to enlist with Dmitri. Two Jesuits also speak up—in Latin—but they are seized, for though they are on Dmitri's side, the vagabond priests have no use for Jesuits. The blood lust of the crowd is aroused, and they drag away the Jesuits to be hanged. When Dmitri rides in on a noble white horse, sumptuously attired,

he is the very picture of a rescuing hero. He proclaims that
he is their true Tsar, adds the usual campaign promises, and
invites them to follow him to the Kremlin where, as the
rightful heir, he will seize the throne from the usurper Boris.
They follow—including the Jesuits—singing, "Glory, hail to
thee, Dmitri." Trumpets and church bells announce that the
town is Dmitri's.

Only the simpleton is left on the scene. Sitting alone on a
stone, he wails a prophecy that is immensely touching in its
combination of wisdom and childlike simplicity. "Weep, ye
people, soon the foe shall come, soon the gloom shall fall.
Woe to our land! Weep, Russian folk, weep, hungry folk."

Weep, indeed. The curtain falls.

Like most composers, Mussorgsky had to endure much trav-
ail; *Boris* did not leap to instant success. The version heard
today is generally not the one he wrote at white heat and played
eagerly for his friends, having worked at it from October 1868
to December 1869. Much excitement and some praise attended
a private presentation of several scenes. He was emboldened
thereby to submit the score to the Committee of the Imperial
Theater, whose approval was necessary. In July 1870 he wrote
resignedly to Rimsky-Korsakov, "I am to be summoned some-
time after August 15, but *They* cannot stage anything new
this year."

On the day that the Committee was to make its decision,
Yulia Platonova, an actress who greatly admired the composer,
gave a luncheon, to which she invited his friend Ludmila
Shestakova—Glinka's sister—and also the conductor Eduard Nápravnik and the stage manager Kondratyev. The two gentlemen
had attended the Committee meeting, and arrived late. Ludmila's
first question was, "Is *Boris* accepted?" Nápravnik shook his

head. "No," he replied. "It's impossible for an opera to have no female element. Let him insert one more scene, then *Boris* will be presented." Ludmila sent a messenger to Mussorgsky, urgently inviting him and his friend Vladimir Stasov to come to her at six o'clock that evening. She then broke the news as tactfully as she could. Undaunted, Mussorgsky immediately started to talk about how he could improve the work. He seated himself at the piano, played and sang various new themes, with Stasov and Ludmila applauding and approving, until midnight.

Ludmila took a special interest in *Boris,* for it was in her living room that Professor Vladimir Nikolsky suggested the Pushkin play to Mussorgsky. It was she who sent him Pushkin's *Boris Godunov,* with blank pages she had inserted so that he might write the libretto and at the same time refer to the play. When his first revision was finished, Mussorgsky sent the book back to her, inscribed:

Here you have, dear Ludmila Ivanova, the completion of
the labors of which you have been witness.

27th January, 1871
Modest Mussorgsky

The book is one of the treasures of the Russian Public Library in Leningrad.

It is not strictly true that the absence of sex interest was the only factor against acceptance by the Imperial Theater. The emphasis on the Tsar's guilt and the People's rebellion could not have been acceptable in imperial circles. The events of sixteenth-century Russia were not that far removed from those of the nineteenth century. In fact, Tsar Alexander II was assassinated three days after Mussorgsky died, in 1881. Furthermore, the music was pronounced "bleak," its conversational idiom "stark," and its magnificent arias not enough to make up for its defects.

He worked hard at the revision, wherever he happened to be living. At first, he stayed on his brother's estate, but in 1869 that had to be sold, and he moved in for a while with Nadezhda and Alexandra Purgold. The latter was married, so the arrangement was perfectly respectable. As a bachelor, Modest moved about easily and was welcome everywhere. His salary from the small job in the Forestry office obtained for him by Stasov was enough to keep him alive. In 1871 he and Rimsky-Korsakov took an apartment together. "Modinka" was thirty-two, "Kosinka" twenty-seven. Stasov came over often to rout them out of bed in the morning. They would breakfast together on tea and rolls and bacon and eggs. "How good it all was!" reminisced Stasov. The two composers shared the piano amicably, each taking his turn when the other was busy. Their close association is important because "Kosinka" heard much of the third act of *Boris* while "Modinka" was hammering it out. Although he deplored his friend's unorthodox methods, he could not help admiring the crude grandeur of the product. It was right, then, that he should have been the one to edit the score when fifteen years after Modest's death *Boris Godunov* was revived.

The jolly bachelor arrangement came to an end when "Kosinka" married Nadezhda Purgold. But before this, there was a performance of the revised *Boris* at Nadezhda's, which Borodin pronounced "a delight! Such variety! Such contrasts! How rounded off and motivated it all is now!" But the Committee did not agree, and again rejected the revised score. Not until January 27, 1874, was the opera finally presented. *"Nyet"* growled some critics, *"Da,"* applauded the public. His friends tried to bring a laurel wreath to the stage for him at this performance. The authorities forbade it. His erstwhile friend César Cui launched an attack which could have been dictated only by envy and malice. He stated that the libretto was feeble, the tone painting crude, and he deplored its immaturity, lack of technique, and Wagnerism. Mussorgsky had remarked that "Wagner is powerful in that he lays hands on art and yanks it around." He believed that this was a good thing, but his way of yanking was his own, wholly original. In no way did it resemble Wagner's.

There were twenty-one performances of *Boris* in the seven years that remained of the composer's life. When it was revived in 1896, with the great Feodor Chaliapin as Boris, Rimsky-Korsakov had applied cosmetics to its rugged features. He ruefully confessed that he both loved and hated *Boris*. "I worship it for its originality, boldness, power, independence, and beauty. I hate it for its shortcomings, the roughness of its harmonies, the incoherencies in the music." His smoothed-out version is the one that is generally given. Other composers who have tried their hand at editing it are Dmitri Shostakovich and Karol Rathaus. The famous Russian basso Boris Christoff —as well as Chaliapin—gave memorable performances of *Boris*. At the Metropolitan Opera in New York, George London, Cesare Siepi, and Jerome Hines covered themselves with glory in the demanding title role. The original score, edited by Paul Lamm and published by Sergei Koussevitzky and Josif Jorgensen in 1928, has threatened to become a museum piece, neglected and forgotten. Yet in June 1971, Gian-Carlo Menotti had the gumption to unearth it for a performance at the Spoleto Festival in Italy. He called it "an intimate *Boris*." Its simplicity and clarity of line were so markedly characteristic of Mussorgsky as to make the Rimsky-Korsakov version sound overfussy and ponderous. It conveyed the sense of turbulence, of overwhelming power, of massive drive that Mussorgsky intended, and that made *Boris Godunov* the greatest of all Russian operas.

RECORDINGS*

Christoff, Lear, Cluytens, Paris Cons. Orch., Cho.   4-Angel S-3633
Excerpts from above   Angel S-36169
London, Melik-Pashayev, Bolshoi Th.   4-Columbia MS-696
Vishnevskaya, Ghiaurov, Spiess, Talvela, Maslennikov, Karajan,
    Vienna Phil.   4-London 1439
Kleptaskaya, Shulpin, Petrov, Mishutin, Melik-Pashayev, Bolshoi
    Th. (selections)   Melodiya/Angel S-40049

Bugarinovich, Changolovich, Baranovich, Belgrade Nat'l Op. Orch.
                                              3-Richmond 63020
Golovanov, Bolshoi Th.   3-Period 1033
Leskaya, Tamarin, Kipnis, Berezowsky, Victor Sym. Orch. & Cho.
    (selections)   RCA Victrola 1396
Reizen, Nebolsin (selections)   Monitor 2016

* Taken from Schwann-1 Record & Tape Guide, February 1973, and from Schwann-2 Record & Tape Guide, Spring 1973.

Bizet's

CARMEN

BIZET'S

Carmen

There were two joint impresarios of the Opéra-Comique in Paris of the early 1870s. One was Camille du Locle, a gay, witty, satirical man-about-town who fancied himself as a critic and writer. He tried to put his personal imprint on the light-opera productions he offered—particularly the dramatic aspects, for he did not know or care too much about music. The other was Adolphe de Leuven, a tall, conservative aristocrat of the old school, son of the Count von Ribbing who had fled to France from Sweden on account of his involvement in the murder of the democratic King Gustav III eighty years before. (The old Count appears in Verdi's *A Masked Ball* under the odd name of Samuele.) De Leuven did not know too much about music either, but he liked to hold to the pleasant standards suggested by the name of his old theater—the Opéra-Comique—and present tuneful musical comedies with happy endings. He had even written librettos for a number of them. Light music, spoken dialogue, and generally happy endings had been the policy of the house ever since it first opened its doors in 1715 on the Rue Favart.

It was du Locle who in 1871 had commissioned the thirty-three-year-old Georges Bizet to compose a one-act opera named *Djamileh*. The quite undramatic libretto was based on a poem by Alfred de Musset entitled *Namouna*. Du Locle changed the title to *Djamileh*, just because he liked to put his finger into every pie and because he had run across the name on a visit to the Near East, where the story is set. Another composer had had the libretto on his desk for six months before du Locle became impatient, took it away from him, and turned it over to Georges Bizet with instructions to write the score at once, if not sooner. Bizet finished the entire work, including the orchestration, in less than two months. At the same time, he was working on another opera, which was never completed, and on a series of piano pieces, which were.

Djamileh was not a success. Bizet himself put it succinctly and accurately a few moments before the curtain descended on the premiere. He whispered to the librettist sitting beside him in the prompter's box: "Now *there's* a complete flop!" The audience and a majority of the critics thoroughly agreed. So, apparently, did the management of the Opéra-Comique, for after eleven performances it was withdrawn and not revived at that theater till 1938, fifty-six years after its premiere. It was no overwhelming success then, either.

Yet there were those who thought it an excellent work, particularly those who really knew their business. Ernest Reyer, a well-established opera composer as well as a critic, wrote an extremely favorable review. Jules Massenet sent Bizet a detailed and enthusiastic letter on the merits of *Djamileh*. Camille Saint-Saëns composed a sonnet on the idiocy of the public in not appreciating *Djamileh*. And Bizet himself, always an honest and perceptive self-critic, was happy with what he had done: he thought that after four other failures, or near failures, he had at last broken through and learned how good operas should be written.

Du Locle and de Leuven too must have seen some of the merits of the work. At least they fully understood that those who really knew what they were talking about—especially composers —considered Bizet something of a genius and certainly the coming man. Whatever their reasoning, before *Djamileh* had run its full eleven performances, they signed him to a contract for a full-length opera. Not only that, but they offered him the services of the most successful writing team in town to do the libretto—Henri Meilhac and Ludovic Halévy. And to show that they truly meant business, they offered him, also, synopses of three comedies from any one of which the writers would work out a libretto at his command. Finally, should he not approve of any of them, he could suggest any other story.

Bizet was, naturally, delighted with this convincing vote of confidence. He was delighted to receive the assignment; he was delighted with the librettists, one of whom, Halévy, was his wife's cousin. He was, however, not delighted with the synopses. He had no objection to writing an opéra comique with dialogue, something with a bright, colorful background—"gay" was the word used in the discussions. But this time he wanted a subject with more drama than, say, something called "The Bluebird," which was one of the subjects offered.

Finally he chose a short novel he had long admired. Its name was "Carmen."

II.   "I BEG OF YOU, DO NOT LET HER DIE!"

When, in 1872, Bizet chose Prosper Mérimée's *Carmen* for the source of his next opera, the book was already a quarter-century-old classic, its author just two years dead. He had been considered one of the greatest masters of French prose and is still studied in the secondary schools of France and many other countries.

Mérimée had been an archeologist, historian, novelist, diplomat, linguist, and cynic. His short novel would scarcely seem to be promising material for a comic opera, especially not one which the managers of the Opéra-Comique expected to be not only a comedy, but also a bright, gay, happy stage piece. Most of the novel's scenes take place in dark, dismal spots, and it is filled with death and violence.

Mérimée wrote it in the first person after being in Spain on an archeological trip where he met, in a cave, a young deserter from the army who was being sought by the police on a charge of murder. The deserter's name was José Lizarrobengoa, and he looked, said Mérimée, like Milton's Satan—implying a dignity and beauty that very few operatic tenors are favored with. Mérimée was attracted to the man and some time later, when he met him again in a tavern with the police close on his trail, helped him escape.

The last Mérimée saw of José was in a prison cell. He had been condemned to be hanged the next morning, and he told his whole story to his French friend. In outline and in its two principal characters—José and Carmen—the story is the same as the one in the opera, which we will presently examine in detail. It is the story of a soldier obsessed with his passion for an infinitely fascinating gypsy woman incapable of faithfulness. When she inevitably falls out of love with him, he is driven to killing her. But in the details, in actual events, in all the minor characters, what a difference! How much darker and more vicious is the story as Mérimée tells it than it is on the stage. Yet, oddly enough, in some respects the brighter operatic version becomes, by the same token, more dramatic. For instance: José kills Carmen, in the novel, in a dark valley and then buries her there silently as she had wished. In the opera, he kills her on a bright plaza in Seville right outside the bullring where her new lover is triumphing in the ring. We hear the shouts of the crowd, and as they come out of the arena, the broken-hearted murderer gives himself up. That, in the opera, is, so far as we know, the only time José has ever killed anyone. In Mérimée's story, which covers many more months than the opera's, José is first driven to other acts of violence. They include a fatal duel with Carmen's rather horrible one-eyed husband (she is un-married in the opera) and the near murder of an Englishman whose mistress she had once been. And Carmen picks the vic-tim's pocket. As for the smugglers, who lend lightness and wit to the opera, they are, in Mérimée, serious and rather dour practitioners of their trade. That lighthearted comic figure, Le Remendado, for instance, is wounded, in Mérimée, by the sol-diery, and Carmen's husband finishes him off with six shots in the face so that he won't be recognized.

Mérimée is classified in histories of French literature as "ro-mantic," but these few details show well why the purveyors of comedy at the Opéra-Comique did not think that his story would fit very well among the romantic bonbons which their theater regularly offered the good, middle-class Parisian bon-bon-eaters in the early days of the Third Republic.

De Leuven was especially scandalized. He pleaded with Halévy when the libretto was barely begun and, according to the librettist himself, spoke like this:

"Isn't she assassinated by her lover? At the Opéra-Comique! A family theater! A theater for the promotion of marriages! We rent five or six boxes every night for these meetings of young couples. You are going to put our audiences to flight. No, it's impossible. Please, I beg you, do not let Carmen die. Death has never been seen on this stage, do you hear, never! Don't let her die, I beg of you, my dear child."

Halévy tried to reassure the old gentleman. They were going to introduce a nice, pure, blond heroine—José's village sweetheart, who is barely alluded to in Mérimée. The gypsy smugglers would be gay and comical. Even the death scene would be "sneaked in at the end of a very lively, brilliant act played on a holiday in bright sunlight with triumphal processions and joyous fanfares."

De Leuven reluctantly gave in. But even as Halévy was leaving, he called once more after him: "Please try not to have her die! Please!"

Halévy could not for a moment have seriously considered saving Carmen's life. Even if he had, he knew perfectly well that Bizet would never have agreed: it would ludicrously have ruined the inevitable point of the story. But de Leuven had not really been won over. Six months after this interview he resigned his directorship of the Opéra-Comique largely, it is said, because of the upcoming production of *Carmen*. Du Locle had given his consent even before Halévy's interview with de Leuven, but reluctantly too. He did not much care for the story then or later, but at least it was a novelty. He liked novelties.

III.   CREATING A MASTERPIECE BETWEEN INTERRUPTIONS

Although Bizet had received his commission in 1872 to write the opera that turned out to be *Carmen*, he did not complete the score till late in 1874, and it was produced only the following spring. This unusually long delay had nothing to do with laziness or inefficiency, for composer and librettists were all conscientious and efficient workers—especially Bizet. There were interruptions because of the shaky state of the Opéra-Comique's finances and some doubts about its ability to survive. In actual fact, not too long after *Carmen*, du Locle failed and had to sell out. But one may find better reasons for the comparatively long time from conception to birth by taking a glance at Bizet's private and professional life during those years.

At the time he received the commission, Bizet was in a state of euphoria because his witty, pretty, sometimes charming, flirtatious, neurotic wife Geneviève was pregnant. More than ever, he felt it incumbent on him to earn money. Even before his son was born in July, Bizet began work on the incidental music for Daudet's tragic play *L'Arlésienne*. It was completed that summer, produced in October, and turned out, as its author put it, "a dazzling failure." Bizet, however, at once extracted a suite of pieces for full orchestra from it, and this was very successful in concerts. Indeed, it still is. The *L'Arlésienne* Suite No. 1 remains, after *Carmen*, the most popular of all of Bizet's music.

The success of the *L'Arlésienne* Suite led to a commission for a concert overture. This he composed quickly, calling it *La Patrie* but never indicating which particular fatherland he had in mind. A rousing, march-like piece, it was an even greater success than the suite and stayed in the repertoire of French orchestras for years. Today it is seldom played or thought of.

During this time, while Bizet was slowly evolving *Carmen*, he also gave literally hundreds of piano lessons at twenty francs for half an hour. According to one American girl who studied with him, he was a formally polite bear when he came to her home, cold and utterly frightening. He would wander around the room or stare at a picture while she performed a piece she had slaved over, apparently paying no attention. Yet, though he might have his back turned, he would stop her, not merely for a wrong note, but for an error in fingering. Promptly at the end of the half hour he would leave, as often as not forgetting either the fee that had been left on a table for him, or else his hat.

But when the lessons were at his own home, he was completely charming and, what with talk and coffee and bonbons, they might last all afternoon. The lessons took place in the parlor, where the grand piano was; but every once in a while, Bizet would disappear into his studio, where he had a piano built into a writing table. From the parlor, the student would hear the master working out some passage or theme he had, apparently, just thought of. She did not know it then, but later realized it was material for *Carmen*.

Carmen it may have been. But it also might have been *Don Rodriguez*. For in the summer of 1873 he sketched out the vocal parts of an entire five-act opera entitled *Don Rodriguez*, which he wrote for Jean-Baptiste Faure, the leading baritone of the principal opera house in France, the Paris Opéra. He performed the entire work, taking all the vocal parts and playing the accompaniment from memory, for Faure and the librettists, who were enormously impressed. Then a typical bit of Bizet luck occurred. Before Faure could get the work accepted, the Paris Opéra burned down. Those vocal parts still exist, but only in manuscript.

Nor were composition and piano lessons Bizet's only musical occupations during the years that he was working on *Carmen*. Early in 1873 the Opéra-Comique introduced its audiences to Gounod's *Romeo and Juliet*, thus belying de Leuven's claim that "death has never been on this stage." As everyone knows, Juliet, like Carmen, dies by dagger in full view of the audience. Gounod, who was living in London in marital exile at the time, asked that his former pupil supervise the production for him, and Bizet attended no fewer than fifty rehearsals.

In addition to all this, there were family troubles. His widowed mother-in-law, whom he both liked and admired, was perhaps even more neurotic than her daughter Geneviève, and made both practical and emotional demands on her son-in-law which he found difficult to meet. As for Geneviève herself, she became more and more neurasthenic after the birth of her son, and it looked for a time as though the marriage might break up permanently. For three months the Bizets were separated, Geneviève going to live with a cousin, Bizet remaining in the Paris apartment, frequently suffering from attacks of the throat quinsy that habitually followed emotional crises.

Despite so much musical work, despite so much emotional distraction, Bizet worked at Carmen, when he could, with the greatest inspiration and most meticulous care. He worked not only on the music but on the libretto as well. When he did not feel that the words his librettists supplied him with exactly hit off the character who was to sing them, he would send them back explaining just what he wanted, and if the new version was still not entirely satisfactory, he would write his own. Between revisions in words and music, Carmen's first-act number, the "Habanera," was completely rewritten eighteen times.

That number also illustrates his attitude toward writing a "Spanish" opera. An equally conscientious but less imaginative, less practical man than Bizet, who wanted to write a "Spanish" opera like Carmen, might be expected to visit Spain, or at least make a thorough study of its folk music. Not Bizet. He was through and through a Frenchman writing for French audiences, and he must have known that his task was to project a Frenchman's idea of Spain and that he would fail if he posed, on the basis of dry research, as a genuine Spaniard. Had he wished to be scholarly, he could scarcely have chosen a melody that, by its very title, "La Habanera," must have come from Cuba and not from Spain. Apparently he heard the song somewhere, thought it to be a genuine folk song, and adapted it for his own purposes. Only when it was already in the opera did he discover that the version he had heard had already been published by a Spanish composer named Sebastián Yradier. Bizet, in his conscientious fashion, acknowledged this fact in the published score.

There is, of course, other Spanish music in *Carmen*—the "Seguidilla," a dance form, in Act I, the dance, based on a *pollo*, that opens Act II, and so forth; but there is surprisingly little music in the score traceable directly to Spain. The only remaining evidence of Bizet's making any effort to be scholarly is a request to the library of the Paris Conservatoire for any book of Spanish songs they might have. They had just one, and Bizet did not use it.

The care and conscientiousness went rather into making every melody, every note, express precisely what he knew it should express. The "Habanera," as we have seen, he rewrote eighteen times. But to get what turned out to be the best-known melody of all—the so-called "Toreador Song"—he tore up the original aria he had written for the Toreador's introduction and substituted the bouncy, cheerful tune that so well epitomizes the tough, good-natured bull-butcher. Later in the opera, Bizet transforms the tune for strikingly dramatic purposes. It simply cannot be true, as one famous conductor of the time claimed, that Bizet contemptuously characterized the tune as "excrement." He made far too much use of it.

By the spring of 1874—that is, two years after he had given the commission—du Locle informed Bizet that he wanted to go into production that fall. Bizet, by this time, was all but ready with the opera, excepting the orchestration. Geneviève had returned to him, and he packed up the family for a summer in a suburb. There, within a space of two months, he worked out one of the subtlest yet clearest and most original orchestrations any opera had ever had. At the end of two months he was able to show the completed full score of his masterpiece—twelve hundred pages, twenty-six staves to a page, in his small, tidy musical handwriting. Just copying that much in that time, let alone creating a marvel, would have been a considerable accomplishment.

IV.   PUTTING THE PIECES TOGETHER

Du Locle had finally scheduled the premiere for October of 1874, and the score was finished in time. But—again for financial reasons—it had to be put off to the following spring. This disappointment gave Bizet more time for a task he relished—to pass judgment on the qualifications of the singer to be chosen for the role of Carmen. The librettists suggested a light soprano named Zelma Bouffer, who had had considerable success in the light confections of Jacques Offenbach. But even before Bizet could interview her, du Locle turned her down as unsuitable for the role. Then an approach was made to Marie Rôze, a very charming, very proper, and very successful operatic soprano. She had a friendly visit with the composer, was made politely to understand that Carmen would not be cleaned up for her temperament, sang a bit for the young maestro, and later wrote an engaging letter saying that he was quite right to keep Carmen "scabrous," that she certainly did not fit the part. Anyway she had wanted to meet him and have him hear her sing and express a favorable opinion—which he had done *after* they agreed the part of Carmen was not for her.

Finally du Locle sent to Bizet the singer so obviously suited for the role that one can only wonder today why he had not asked her in the first place. Her name was Célestine Galli-Marié, a mezzo-soprano, unlike the first two, who were sopranos. She was dark, and though she was born in Paris, there seems to have been about her the aura of a Spanish gypsy. One critic, reviewing her in a comedy, wrote, "She is small and graceful, moves like a cat, has an impish, pert face, and her whole personality seems unruly and mischievous." Like Carmen, she knew precisely what she wanted: she wanted to "create" the role and dealt forthrightly with du Locle about her fees, compromising only when it became apparent that without compromise she would have to give it up. But when, during rehearsals, the management wanted her and Bizet to tone down the "scabrous" aspects of the role, she put her foot down firmly. Loyal to the composer and her art, she acted the role with all the sexiness and abandon at her command, which, according to many reports, was very considerable.

When she first met Bizet to have him play her the score, she was thirty-three, already a widow for over ten years, and had been a leading mezzo in various European theaters since she was nineteen. Though she had many roles in her repertoire, she was chiefly identified with the part of Mignon in Ambroise Thomas' highly successful opera. Later on she was to become even more famous as Carmen. Bizet saw, almost at once, that he had found the ideal impersonator for his colorful heroine. He also, apparently, decided that she was a very attractive woman. But though she regarded him as a dear friend and fully understood his genius, she was careful, in the friendliest but firmest manner possible, to avoid the extra private coaching sessions he suggested. There was backstage gossip about them, of course. There always is backstage gossip. But Galli-Marié was very much a woman of the world. She knew that, as an opera singer, she could "respectably" maintain a ménage with a rising young composer named Émile Paladilhe (who was four years younger than herself) but not at the same time become the mistress of another (who was two years older).

Yet that there was some sort of affinity between Bizet and his gypsy-like prima donna is attested to by a well-authenticated story—at least for those who believe in telepathy. On the night that Bizet died in the country, Galli-Marié was performing *Carmen* on the stage of the Opéra-Comique. During the third act, while she reads death in the cards, a dreadful feeling came over her, and at the end of the act she completely collapsed. When she came out of her faint, du Locle sympathetically asked her what the matter was and whether she was better. "Nothing is the matter with me," she said. "Nothing. But something dreadful is happening." And she went back, like a good trouper, and sang Act IV. But the next day, when she heard that Bizet had died the night before, she developed a high fever. That night there was no *Carmen*.

Finally, late in 1874, rehearsals actually did get started, and they went on daily for several months. For *Carmen* seemed to the performers of the day, and to the management as well, a radical and difficult work. The orchestra rebelled, claiming that much of it was "unplayable." The women of the chorus were especially grieved. Normally, in the works performed at the Opéra-Comique, the chorus came out all together, lined up, and kept their eyes glued to the conductor as they sang. In *Carmen*, they come on in twos and threes; they are expected to *act* (perish the thought!) and even fight while they are singing. Worst of all, they must smoke cigarettes, which the women objected to on three grounds—they didn't know how; it was an immoral thing to do, especially in public; it made them sick. (Over twenty-five years later, in a production in Kansas City, these objections prevailed. The cigarette factory was changed to a dairy, and the girls came on carrying milk pails.)

Nor was du Locle much help. Though he remained on the friendliest of terms with Bizet, whom he seemed to like rather in spite of than because of his genius, he called the music incomprehensible. He tried, working largely through the librettists, to get the action to look more polite, but Galli-Marié's resistance was loyally seconded by her leading tenor, Paul Lhérie. Fearful of a scandal, du Locle let it be generally known that *Carmen* might prove to be quite a shocker and even invited a prominent politician to view a dress rehearsal to judge for himself whether he wanted to bring his family. Today such behavior might be viewed as shrewd publicity-seeking. Not in Paris of the 1870s. For *Carmen* du Locle even neglected to indulge in the subtle bribery of critics which the venal press of the day considered routine.

Bizet himself was not especially worried by what he heard of rumors. He paid attention strictly to musical matters, and when he deemed an extra six sopranos and mezzos absolutely necessary for the chorus, did not hesitate to ask du Locle for them. And the impresario, though he was already in precarious financial straits gave in reluctantly. Bizet was sure that he had written a masterpiece, that *Carmen* would permanently change the milk-and-water character of the opéra comique form. He coached and drilled his performers so enthusiastically that before opening night most of them had come around to his way of thinking. The opera was still strange to them—but wonderful.

But the anticipatory attitude of the public was better re-

flected in the circumstance that the government announced on
the morning of the premiere that Bizet had been awarded the
Legion of Honor. A typical Parisian sneerer thereupon remarked: "They announced it this morning because they knew
that after tonight it would no longer be possible to give him any
decoration."

V.   DOES CRITICISM KILL?

The premiere on the night of March 3, 1875, started well
enough—even brilliantly. The audience included famous composers—Gounod, Thomas, Offenbach, Delibes (Saint-Saëns came
to a later performance)—as well as writers—Alphonse Daudet
and his brother Ernest among them—critics, music publishers,
men of the world who rather hoped for the scandal the news-
papers had hinted that they might expect. But there was no
scandal, no demonstration. The first act was most enthusiastically
received, especially the "Habanera" and the soprano-tenor duet.
During the intermission, Bizet welcomed hearty and sincere congratulations on the stage from the many sincere and insincere
"friends" he numbered among his acquaintances. The second act
started even better. The quiet and simple tune played before the
curtain goes up so enchanted the audience that it had to be re-
peated, and the "Toreador Song" with chorus, which comes near
the beginning of the act, made a stunning effect.

Then the reaction began to cool off in what might be called
an almost unrelieved decrescendo. Far fewer well-wishers
showed up during the intermission. Only the third-act soprano
aria briefly stemmed the descent into coldness or apathy. At that
point, according to a teen-ager sitting with him, Gounod, Bizet's
former teacher and beloved mentor, stood up in the front of his

box and applauded vigorously for all to see. Then he sat down again remarking, "That melody is mine. Georges has robbed me. Take the Spanish tunes and mine out, and there's nothing remaining to Georges' credit." . . . "That," concluded the boy, "after all those embraces on the stage, was my first lesson in duplicity." After that act, Bizet did not bother to go to the stage. He paced the sidewalk outside the opera house nervously and replied sadly to an admirer's embarrassed compliments. "I foresee a hopeless flop." Just what he had said of *Djamileh*.

The last act was the most hopeless flop of all. It seems difficult to believe today, but all the accounts agree that that most exciting murder, both dramatically and musically in all of opera, elicited nothing more than a polite spattering of applause, after which the audience quietly filed out. The premiere inspired neither a scandalous demonstration, as some had hoped, nor enthusiasm, as some knew it merited. Just failure. Nor could the performance be blamed. True, there were two mishaps. José, performing his little ditty offstage, went way off key, and at one point, while Carmen was singing a soft passage, the tympanist, having miscounted his bars of rest, came in with two mighty blows. But on the whole, it was agreed that the principals, and especially Galli-Marié, sang and acted with spirit and conviction. Even the chorus girls smoked without mishap.

But failure this time, as it never had before, seemed to affect Bizet at once with a deep gloom. His immediate reaction was to retire in silence to du Locle's office and then to walk through the streets of Paris for hours in the company of his close friend, the composer Ernest Guiraud, and complain bitterly. He could not seek consolation from Geneviève. Rather ill, she had not attended the premiere. Besides, their relationship was still a difficult one.

Most of the reviewers jumped to the attack as if they had

been paid to do so. The principal complaint was against the sordid story, the fact that there was not one decent character in the whole work excepting only Micaela, the sweet, innocent blonde Halévy had promised to de Leuven. Carmen herself came in for dithyrambs of dispraise as "a veritable prostitute of the gutter and the crossroads," and one critic went so far as to suggest that the "distinguished artist" who assumed the part performed it in such a lascivious fashion that she might, perhaps, share some of that character. Bizet was especially upset by this innuendo, but it is not recorded what Galli-Marié said. One rather suspects that this worldly wise woman felt both amused and complimented on her art.

Nor was the music spared by these gentlemen of the press. It was excoriated by some for being too Wagnerian and by others for not being Wagnerian enough. The score was also attacked for lack of melody (*what, no tunes in Carmen?*), for having the melodies sounded only in the orchestra while the singers bawled something else (that is what was meant by Wagnerism), for its failure to use enough Spanish folk songs.

There was also a minority of favorable notices, but these were not a great deal more knowledgeable than the others. In addition, he received several congratulatory notes from men who knew their business, like the composers Delibes and Saint-Saëns. Only one critic went to the trouble—and had the insight—to write, for a magazine, a long and remarkably perceptive evaluation of the merits of the score. But by this time Bizet had been so battered by the reception of what he thought was to be his "break-through" opera that he kept repeating, "Perhaps they are right." He acknowledged the critique that should really have heartened him only with a brief note saying, "Thank you for your charming piece." And on one occasion Bizet acted as his extreme pride and self-control had never permitted him to do before. He met one of the fiercest critics of *Carmen* in the street and thoroughly berated him. The critic defended himself and his right to his opinions, whereupon Bizet pulled himself together and walked away.

Outwardly he fought off his depression, even though his apparent defeat continued to rankle. He must have been encouraged by a long letter from a friend who attended the second performance of *Carmen* two nights after the first and reported not only the pleasure it had given himself but the great enthusiasm of the audience. He must also have been encouraged by du Locle's offer, a short time after the premiere, of a contract for another opéra comique to be written with the same librettists, Meilhac and Halévy. He was still too discouraged with opéra comique to accept this offer, but he did discuss, with a librettist, his plans for an oratorio on the subject of St. Geneviève of Paris. He took pains in going over the score of a new opera a friend brought around for his criticism; he went over the score of *Carmen* for the benefit of a new young singer, and then asked her to sing Schumann songs for him. Such friends and acquaintances were delighted with his company, as almost everyone had always been; but later on they recalled how ill he had looked, how his hearing in one ear seemed to have weakened. And they recalled that after the Schumann songs, Bizet had sat down at the piano and played not one but two funeral marches.

He was put to bed with one of the throat infections that customarily attacked him when he was emotionally disturbed, and he fell down one day after getting out of bed from the sheer pain of the rheumatism he had developed. Recovering slightly, he decided that he could feel well again only in the country and toward the end of May moved his family to Bougival, the suburb where he had completed the score of *Carmen*. He at once felt better and rashly took a cold swim in the Seine. Two days after that a severely painful attack of rheumatism all but paralyzed him, and after another two days, he suffered a heart attack. A local doctor stayed with him most of the night and then assured the family that the crisis was over and Bizet perfectly safe. Bizet knew better. The next night, toward twelve, he suffered another heart attack. He did not call his wife but, significantly, the housekeeper, who had served his mother for years before she died. He told her he knew that this was the end and fell into a coma. Before the doctor could get there, at about 3 A.M., he was dead.

That was on June 3, 1875, the morning after the thirty-third performance of Carmen, the one at which Galli-Marié fainted.

Did the failure of *Carmen* kill its composer? It used to be fashionable to say so. But matters of life and death are seldom so simply explained as that. One can count off too many other contributing factors to accept easily so simplified and romantic a thesis. Bizet's ruddy complexion and stocky build made him look deceptively healthy, but throughout his life he was subject to debilitating illnesses, especially to the painful throat infections with their accompanying abscesses. His financial troubles caused him to overwork. The deep disappointment with the way his marriage was working out—though we do not know much about it—must constantly have gnawed at him in the last two years of his life. No, one cannot blame the critics alone. Still, it is probable that had *Carmen* been received as it deserved to be, Bizet would have lived longer than a pitiful thirty-seven years. And composed more than one masterpiece.

VI.   FROM FAILURE TO FAME

Was that first production of *Carmen* really a failure? Thirty-seven performances played in ninety-three days by a repertory company would rather seem to indicate success. By comparison it looks even better when one learns that during those months du Locle put on two other new works—one of them by Émile Paladilhe, Galli-Marié's lover. That one lasted through only six performances, the other through ten. And *Carmen* went on, during its first year, to a total of fifty performances. Nevertheless, it must be accounted a failure with the Parisians of the day. The house was seldom more than half full and often less than that. The only success poor du Locle had that season was a series of seven sold-out performances of Verdi's *Requiem,* the composer conducting. The failure of his principal attraction—*Carmen*—along with ill health were the real reasons du Locle was forced to sell out. *Carmen* did not return to the stage of the Opéra-Comique for eight years.

The day before he died, Bizet signed a contract for a production in Vienna. *Carmen* was produced there four months later with spectacular success. From that time on it has never ceased to be one of the most popular operas in the entire world, not only with the general public, but with the greatest of composers and with other prominent figures. Wagner, who happened to be visiting Vienna, exclaimed, "Here at last, thank God, is someone with ideas in his head!" Brahms, whose home was Vienna, attended twenty performances and said he would have gone to the ends of the earth to embrace Bizet. Friedrich Nietzsche, though some years later, in *The Case of Wagner* wrote pages of praise of *Carmen* as a stick to beat his former friend. He, too, had prepared himself by attending twenty performances. Chancellor Bismarck, no mean critic of music, fell under the spell of *Carmen* so completely that, in Berlin, he attended twenty-seven performances. And even before these German authorities had fallen in love with *Carmen,* Tchaikovsky had attended one of the last of the original Opéra-Comique performances, six months after the composer's death. He too fell in love with it, bought a score to study it more closely, proclaimed it a masterpiece, and predicted that within ten years it would be the most popular opera in the world.

Tchaikovsky's prediction proved almost literally true. Within ten years *Carmen's* triumphs were so widespread that a list of the languages it had been given in will best indicate, briefly, how far it had traveled. They include German, Flemish, Hungarian, Italian, Russian, Swedish, English, Czech, Spanish, and Estonian. And the following half century more languages had to be added for the benefit of local enthusiasts. They include Lettish, Dutch, Finnish, Slovenian, Norwegian, Romanian, Serbian, Lithuanian, Ukrainian, Hebrew, and Japanese. That covers the five continents (for it reached Australia, in English, in 1879) but does not even begin to suggest the numbers of productions over the world which have been given in the original French.

Tchaikovsky's enthusiasm was based on hearing and studying the original score in French. The opera as introduced so successfully in Vienna the same year was different in important respects, and some of these changes have generally been retained. It had, of course, been translated into German, but the most important change was that it had been, at least partially, translated from an "opéra comique" into a "grand opera." The technical difference between opéra comique and grand opera is that the former consists of a series of musical numbers interspersed with dialogue which carries on the plot. In nineteenth-century grand opera, there are generally no spoken words at all, and the plot is largely carried on through dialogue set to essentially unmelodic, more or less speech-like notes with orchestral accompaniment, or recitative. Bizet had intended to compose recitatives for the Vienna production, but as he died before he could get to it, the assignment was given to Ernest Guiraud, the close friend with whom he had wandered the streets of Paris after the fiasco of the premiere. Guiraud did not send all the material on time, and so the Vienna premiere used what he had sent and retained a portion of the spoken dialogue. Even so, the occasion was a huge success. Later on, when the balance of the recitatives arrived, Vienna discarded the remainder of the spoken dialogue, and the opera has since generally been both published and performed outside of France— and often in France itself—in the "grand opera" version. Guiraud, however, is seldom credited either on programs or on title pages with his extensive and entirely tasteful contribution.

Another grand opera feature used at Vienna and elsewhere by way of transforming Carmen was the addition of a ballet in Act IV. Grand opera, to be really grand, was expected to give the ballet company at the very least ten minutes to brighten things up. The original version does feature a gypsy dance in Act II, often performed by Carmen and her two gypsy friends, who are expected to sing as they dance. Vienna, and a great many other productions since, have added a much longer ballet in Act IV, as part of the festivities just before the bullfight. There is no singing, and the music most often used comes from Bizet's incidental music to L'Arlésienne.

Much critical ink has been spilled on the question of whether it is better to do the "grand opera version" or the "original." The principal argument in favor of the Opéra-Comique version, with all or most of the original dialogue, is that the necessity of cutting some of that dialogue for musical reasons obscures some of the motivation, especially of minor characters. All kinds of compromises have been tried, most of them successful. In Paris, until the opera was transferred to the Paris Opéra in the late 1960s, it was always given with most, if not all, of the original dialogue. In this form, the opéra comique, on the hundredth anniversary of Bizet's birth, October 25, 1935, it achieved its 2,271st performance at the Opéra-Comique alone. But whether in this form or in "grand opera" form, with ballet or without, the number of performances it has had in many languages and on hundreds of stages must run well into six figures. Its appeal remains so vital that it seems to be impossible to mount a completely uninteresting performance, no matter what the form or who the star is.

For instance, when, by popular demand, the Opéra-Comique reluctantly revived *Carmen* eight years after its initial showing they used musty scenery, rehearsed only the first two acts adequately, and featured a soprano as Carmen who looked and sounded—according to a contemporary critic—like an elephant who had swallowed a canary. The reaction against the production was so violent and the enthusiasm for the opera itself so great, that the management had to make amends swiftly. The role of Carmen, written for a mezzo-soprano, has been sung as well and as often by sopranos, and not infrequently by women with hardly any voice at all. San Francisco's first Carmen was that Mlle. Rôze who had first turned down the role because it was too "scabrous" for her. She was successful. So have been the most refined of singers and also those who made the character as vulgar as they could. The most celebrated of nineteenth-century Carmens—the American Minnie Hauk—sang the role five hundred times, adapting the language to whatever country she was in—French, German, English, or Italian. An-

other American, Geraldine Farrar, who was the Metropolitan
Opera's exclusive Carmen for years, acted it especially well
and made a silent movie of it. So did Theda Bara. Rita
Hayworth made a "talkie," with a dubbed-in voice. The
opera was made a successful rescored musical with a new libretto
and all-Negro cast by Oscar Hammerstein. *Carmen Jones* was
widely successful both on the stage and as a movie. The Russians
transformed the opera into a lively communist musical play
called *Carmencita and the Soldier* and toured the West with it.
Carmen, in various versions, has had television productions seen
by millions both here and abroad. And in 1970 a satirical rock
version, with kazoos and synthesizers, was produced. Inevitably,
in that year, it was called *The Naked Carmen,* but its appeal
was auditory only, for it was a smash-hit record.

The production of *Carmen* which opened the season of
1972–73 at the Metropolitan Opera House in New York was
"different." It created a sensation. Göran Gentele, who had become director of the Metropolitan Opera shortly before his
tragic death, left as a legacy a new interpretation of an old
opera. It enhanced the strength, clarity, and credibility of the
story by using the dialogue Bizet had written into the score, not
the recitatives his friend Guiraud composed to replace it. Guiraud's intentions were strictly honorable. He wanted *Carmen*
to rank as grand opera. Spoken words were not acceptable in
grand opera, and in 1875, they made *Carmen* as déclassé as
its heroine. In 1972 the words did not diminish but rather
enhanced its "grandeur." In that production, moreover, the
heroine as sung by Marilyn Horne was presented, not as a
complete sensualist, but as an earthy, warm-blooded gypsy
whose attraction was so powerful as to drive an honorable soldier
to desert his regiment and ultimately to commit murder. Don
José, as portrayed by James McCracken, was not a stupid peas-

ant, but a man of character led astray by a force beyond his control. The dialogue and the acting threw a new light on the leading characters, on the whole drama, and on the music itself.

For the perfection of its wedding of drama and music, *Carmen* has frequently been called "the perfect opera." Perhaps a more suitable epithet would be "the most durable" or the "inextinguishable." For no matter what imperfections may be visited on its head, what fresh forms it may be given in, it has survived all onslaughts, all "improvements" for over a century and a quarter, and grows greater rather than less in the esteem and love it generates in the minds and hearts of listeners as the quarter centuries keep passing by.

What Happens in

CARMEN

an Opera in Four Acts

Book by

Henri Meilhac and Ludovic Halévy

Music by

Georges Bizet, with recitatives by

Ernest Guiraud

CHARACTERS

[in order of appearance]

Moralès, a corporal	*Baritone or Bass*
Micaela, a peasant girl	*Soprano*
Don José, a corporal	*Tenor*
Zuniga, a lieutenant	*Bass*
Carmen, a gypsy	*Mezzo-soprano or soprano*

Frasquita ⎫
Mercédès ⎬ gypsies
Escamillo, a toreador
El Dancairo ⎫
El Remendado ⎬ smugglers

Soprano
Mezzo-soprano
Baritone
Baritone
Tenor

Time: about 1820
Place: in and near Seville
First performance at Paris, March 3, 1875.

THE STORY AND THE MUSIC

THE PRELUDE

The Prelude to *Carmen* is a masterful, dramatic attention-getter, depicting the tragedy that is to follow contrasted with the bright background against which it will be played. Punctuated with cymbal crashes, the vigorous first theme, associated with the celebration of the bullfight, rings out at once and alternates with the quieter one for the gathering of the crowds before the arena. Then, with a sudden change of key (which was more startling a hundred years ago than it is today), the insouciant, march-like refrain of the Toreador is sung out first softly in the strings, then, loudly, by the whole orchestra. The bullfight music returns; and if Bizet had stopped here, we would have had a perfectly balanced, bright introduction to a comedy about something gay and martial in spirit. Instead, there is a dramatic pause, and the violins attack with a shuddering tremolo. Underneath there enters, in a minor key, the so-called "fate" theme. It is the one used again and again throughout the opera to depict the fateful attraction that the gypsy Carmen exerts on the soldier José. Lest we forget that theme, it is worked up dramatically in the orchestra, exploding on a sharp, unresolved chord. There we are left hanging for a long silence as the curtain rises.

ACT I

On a plaza in Seville, citizens and soldiers are enjoying the noonday sun, the young men awaiting the recess of the girls who work in the cigarette factory on the right, the soldiers lounging outside the guardhouse on the left. In the rear there is a bridge over which other citizens pass on whatever business they have that morning. Corporal Moralès, in the bright yellow and red uniform that made nineteenth-century Spanish soldiers such excellent targets, comments on the attractive scene. Everyone is busy, but all they do is smoke and joke.

Presently the corporal's eye lights on Micaela, a sweet-looking young blonde obviously seeking something or someone in a strange place. Calling the attention of his comrades to the agreeable opportunity, he salutes the girl and asks what she is looking for.

The response is hesitating: "A corporal."

"A corporal? That's me."

"No, I'm afraid it isn't you. His name is Don José."

In a delightful little military tune, Moralès informs the country girl that they all know José, who will be along in a little while when the guard changes. Won't she come and rest in the guardhouse while awaiting him? The other soldiers join in the corporal's urgent pleas, but Micaela has been too well brought up to risk any such adventures and manages to run off, full of embarrassment.

Now a military trumpet call is heard offstage and echoed in the orchestra. In march a bugler and two fifers playing another little march tune, and behind them comes a band of urchins playing at soldiers by marching in ragged formation and singing the tune the fifers have played. Finally comes the new guard headed by Lieutenant Zuniga and Corporal José. While the formal changing of the guard takes place, Moralès tells his fellow corporal of the charming country girl who has been look-ing for him.

José now explains to Zuniga—apparently a newcomer to Se-ville—that the factory girls don't have the purest reputation in the world, but that he himself is not interested—whereupon he deliberately sits down on a chair, his back to the factory, for he knows that the noonday recess is about to bring the girls into the square and he just might be tempted.

The bell sounds, and the knowing young men of the town gather about the factory entrance and frankly announce their intention of making the most of their opportunities. The girls come lazily out, every last one of them smoking (a most im-proper habit for a girl in 1875). They even sing a sinuous melody comparing the quickly disappearing smoke to insincere vows of love. Actually, the men do not pay too much attention to them, for they are awaiting the most attractive girl of all— a gypsy named Carmen. Suddenly she appears, announced in the orchestra by a quick, twisty little theme. Several of the young men immediately surround her.

"Carmen!" they cry, "tell us when you are going to love us!"

"Good Lord," she answers in her characteristic teasing way, "I don't know. Maybe never, maybe tomorrow—but certainly not today."

Thereupon, with the chorus furnishing background, she sings her famous aria, the "Habanera," with the rhythm of a Cuban dance. What too few listeners remember about the words is that they expound her philosophy of love, and that it is this philosophy which inevitably leads to the tragedy. Love, she says, must always be free as a bird and cannot be forced. So if you love me, I won't love you; and I'll love you only if you don't love me. Therefore, loving me can be a very dangerous thing. All of which is not very logical, but she means it.

And she acts on it at once. During the second stanza she notices young José sitting on his chair, whittling away at a piece of wood, earnestly paying her no attention at all. Disconcerted by his continued inattention, she brushes off the young men who renew their pleas after the song and, as the bells sound a back-to-work signal, she takes a rose from her bodice and tosses it directly at him. Everyone laughs at José; the girls return to work; the stage is cleared; and José remains alone on his stool. He leans down to pick up the flower and thrusts it into his tunic. "What a witch!" he mutters.

Now Micaela returns with a message of love, a small bit of money and a kiss from José's mother. They sing a long and very melodious duet about home and mother, and before she leaves, Micaela gives him a letter from the old woman. He reads it and the thought goes through his mind that he has, through the purity of his home, been saved from the wiles of a bad woman. He will return and marry Micaela.

Suddenly there is a great racket in the factory, and the girls come rushing out, calling for soldierly intervention. It seems there has been a violent fight between Carmen and another girl, named Manuelita. They surround Lieutenant Zuniga, half saying Carmen began it all, half blaming the other girl. They even begin fighting among themselves until Zuniga sternly commands silence and orders José, with two privates, to bring out the culprit. Presently José returns leading Carmen, who is in the highest of spirits. She resolutely refuses to answer questions, she flirts with Zuniga, and she repeatedly sings a dancy phrase with the greatest impertinence. The lieutenant is not unmindful of Carmen's attractions, but he thinks on the whole she had better cool off in jail for a while. Commanding José to take her there, he retires to the guardhouse to write out the orders.

While José ties Carmen's hands behind her back and seats her on a chair, she tells him, with complete confidence, that on account of the flower she had thrown him, he is going to help her escape. He tells her gruffly to keep her mouth shut, so she goes to work on him in earnest. Still seated in the chair, her hands still tied, she begins the seductive "Seguidilla." In it, she invites a certain young officer—no lieutenant, only a corporal —to come to the inn of her friend Lillas Pastia to replace her recently dismissed lover. Once again José tries to shush her, but she claims she is only singing a song to herself and thinking. Thinking certainly cannot be forbidden, can it? So she goes on singing "to herself" about what might happen at Lillas Pastia's. Before she is through, she has really got under his skin. Does she truly mean what she promises? Will she love him? Will she be faithful? Yes, of course, says Carmen—and José loosens the cords. Then, triumphantly swinging them, she sings and dances one more stanza of the "Seguidilla," hurrying back to the chair and putting her arms behind her just as Zuniga reappears with the rest of the guard.

Giving José the orders, he warns him that he'd better be careful. Carmen, for her part, manages to whisper instructions to José about how the escape is to be effected, and then turns to Zuniga for a final taunt—a phrase of warning from the "Habanera." José and two soldiers lead her off, and just as they reach the narrow entrance to the bridge, she turns around, gives José a huge shove, and, swinging her cords over her head, dashes away while everyone laughs. Before the curtain falls,

José ruefully picks himself up from the ground and surrenders to Zuniga.

ACT II

There is a short quiet prelude, or entr'acte, based on the jaunty soldier's ditty, "Man of Alcalá" which is sung later in the act by José offstage. Played here first as a bassoon solo, it works its way amiably from minor into major. At the disastrous premiere of the opera, it was the only number to be encored.

Lillas Pastia's inn, on the edge of town, turns out to be a rather low dive, a meeting place for smugglers, but certainly not without charm and gaiety. A lively drinking-and-dancing party is in progress, including Carmen and her two gypsy intimates, Frasquita and Mercédès. Lieutenant Zuniga is prominent in the group of soldiers present, and it is pretty obvious that during the two months since he was first fascinated by her, he has not made much of an impression on her.

A gypsy dance is being performed, and soon Carmen, seconded by Frasquita and Mercédès, is leading the music with the "Gypsy Song." It grows wilder and wilder, and ends with a great climax.

Now, by order of the sheriff, it is closing time, and Zuniga invites the gypsy girls to come along with him. They refuse him, for they have other business. In one last effort to win a smile from Carmen, the lieutenant tells her that the soldier who was put into jail on account of her—meaning, of course, José—has completed his sentence.

"He is free, then? So much the better . . . And now, gentlemen—good night!"

But a chorus of men offstage interrupts them, hailing Esca-

millo, a popular matador who had won a famous victory over a
bull at Granada. He makes a brilliant entrance followed by a
crowd of his fans, and sings the best-known number in the
opera, the "Toreador Song." First he returns a toast offered by
the soldiers and then, with the aid of his cloak, he describes a
bullfight. The familiar refrain ends with the claim that his her-
oism will be rewarded with the love of a dark-eyed beauty. As
the second stanza develops, Escamillo is more and more attracted
by Carmen, and it becomes clear which dark-eyed beauty he
would like for his reward this time. Before leaving the inn, he
asks what her name is and what she would say to an avowal of
love.

"I'd say it would be a waste of time to love me."

"Not exactly a tender answer," remarks Escamillo. "So I'll just
have to wait and hope." Carmen is both amused and attracted.

"There's no law against waiting," she says, "and hope is
sweet."

To Zuniga she is far less encouraging. When the lieutenant
tells her that he is coming back later, she brushes him off with,
"That will be one big mistake." But he makes it, as we shall see.

To the refrain of the "Toreador Song" everyone marches out,
leaving the inn to the three gypsy girls and two leaders of a
band of smugglers, named El Remendado and El Dancairo. The
men tell the girls that there is a plan afoot to smuggle quite a
profitable load of goods across the border but that they will need
womanly wiles to help deal with the guards they are sure to en-
counter. In a completely captivating quintet, the tune tossed
lightly from one singer to another, they all agree with this sen-
timent. Frasquita and Mercédès agree to come along at once, but
Carmen claims that she intends to stay right there. When
pressed for a reason she says she is in love. This makes no sense
to the two men at all. Carmen has been in love often before,

and never yet has failed to combine love and business. She responds in an equally lighthearted fashion, but she remains firm about waiting for José.

At that moment he is heard approaching, singing his soldier's ditty, "Man of Alcalá." El Remendado quickly demands that Carmen get him to join the smuggling party, and to get rid of her companions, she promises at least to try.

José greets Carmen warmly, telling her he has been in prison for two months and would be glad to be there still if it were on her behalf. He shows the lover's signs of jealousy when she tells him that she has been dancing for some of his officers, but she soothes him by preparing to dance for him alone. To the accompaniment of her castanets, she sings a sinuous and wordless melody and dances enticingly around him as he sits fascinated in a chair. Faintly in the distance the bugles sound retreat. José does not notice them at once, but when he does, his automatic reaction is to stop Carmen. She makes believe that she does not understand what the bugles have to do with it. Is he tired, perhaps, of having her dance without accompanying music? She sings, dances, and plays the castanets more vigorously. Again José stops her: he must get back to camp. Now Carmen, like any self-respecting artist interrupted in a performance—or like any pretty girl whose advances are underrated—is really angry.

"Here I've been singing and dancing and, Lord deliver us, I might have loved him pretty soon." (Carmen uses the somewhat cheap device of addressing an imaginary third person.) "Then the bugle sounds—ta-ra-ta-ta—and off he goes. All right, get out, you canary!" (referring to his yellow uniform). She takes his cap, his ammunition box, and his sword and viciously hurls them at him. Piteously he tells her he does not want to go—he loves her—no other woman has ever touched him so. Carmen only grows more irate and thinks of other insults to hurl. Thereupon José's spirits rise too, and he literally forces her to sit quietly in a chair and listen to him. Then he draws from his vest the flower, now faded beyond recognition, that she had thrown him in Act I. In the aria known as the "Flower Song" he tells her how this flower, through all the time he was in prison, somehow kept its fragrance and kept alive his single hope—to see her once again.

Gradually, throughout this beautiful aria, Carmen calms down, and at its close she has been moved by the intense sincerity of José's love. Her first words are, "No, you do not love me," but they are uttered softly, enticingly. He does not love her, for if he did, he would fly with her up to the mountains, to freedom where there are no officers to be obeyed, where their own desires will be their law, where there is only freedom. José, wildly torn between this almost irresistible proposal and his sense of duty, nearly capitulates. He takes her in his arms and is about to kiss her when his sense of honor overwhelms him and he pushes her away.

"Go, then!" cries Carmen. "I hate you!"

"Farewell, then—forever!" cries the broken-hearted José and is about to go when there is a knock at the door. For a moment the two hesitate, and then Lieutenant Zuniga opens it for himself and enters with a sardonic smile.

"Your taste is not very good," he tells Carmen, "taking a plain soldier when you could have had an officer," and he orders José out. José, however, proudly refuses to obey and the two men draw swords. Carmen, delighted to see two men in uniform fighting over her, nevertheless summons help, and gypsies, pouring in from every side, disarm the lieutenant. With utmost politeness, but at the points of two wicked-looking pistols, Dancairo and Remendado invite the lieutenant to leave the premises. With equal Latin polish he admits that their arguments are irresistible and bows out.

His superior officer now a mortal enemy, José has no choice left but to join the gypsies, and the act ends with a joyous chorus in praise of liberty sung to the same melody that Carmen had used in urging José to join them.

ACT III

The Prelude to Act III is a charming little piece not the least bit relevant to the murky third act of *Carmen*. Its principal melody is first softly sung by a solo flute with harp accompaniment, and it bears an accidental resemblance to the opening of the Irish song "The Minstrel Boy." Counter melodies come in, and then the first violins take up the principal theme.

In a clearing in a wild, mountainous region, the rather large smuggling party has gathered its goods in bales preparatory to crossing the border. The gypsies sing a quiet little chorus in a minor key encouraging each other in the somewhat dangerous illegal business they are up to. El Dancairo, their leader, tells them to rest an hour while he and a few others go reconnoitering. Carmen, it becomes clear, has already tired of José, and when he shows some homesickness for his mother (as the orchestra plays), Carmen contemptuously advises him to return where he belongs.

"And be separated from you?" demands José as the fate motive is heard.

"Of course."

"Carmen, I warn you—if you say that again—"

"Then you'll kill me. So what? It's all written in the cards."

Meantime, Frasquita and Mercédès have seated themselves

before a bale and are now busy laying out cards to tell their own fortunes. In a gay, lighthearted duet, Frasquita reports that the cards promise her a fine young lover who takes her up to the mountains, showers her with attentions, and finally becomes a famous leader of a hundred men. Mercédès finds in the cards what she thinks is an even better fate. She is to be wooed by a very rich and very old man who will marry her, present her with diamonds and a castle, and then—best of all—die and leave everything to her.

Presently Carmen spreads out her own pack of cards beside them, but her mood—and her music—are quite different. She lays out first a diamond and then a spade, which she interprets to mean that she will die first and then José. In a slow, ominous, heavy melody she meditates on the vanity of trying to avoid death. The two other women take up their merry tune once more, but Carmen sings only of death, as she continues to turn up spades.

El Dancairo and his reconnoitering party now return and report that it is time to move on. They have spied out three customs officers, but these should be easily handled. In the ensuing march-like chorus, the girls look forward to the task of beguiling these customs officers into neglecting their duties. Only José is to be left behind to mount a nearby hillock and stand guard over the bales of goods not taken on this expedition.

The stage is empty for a few moments when Micaela, left there by a guide, expresses her fear of the ominous surroundings and the possibility of meeting with the awful woman who has seduced her José. Her lovely aria ends with an appeal to heaven to protect her. Her fear turns to fright when she sees José aiming a gun in her general direction, and she runs off to hide behind a huge rock as José shoots.

It is not Micaela, however, whom José has espied climbing up to the smugglers' rendezvous. The Toreador comes in wryly remarking that if the shot had been a few inches lower he would have been done for. José at once descends to challenge him, and it does not take long before he realizes that Escamillo, whom he had never seen before, is there to find Carmen and try to take her from him. The situation demands a fight. The two men wrap cloaks around their left arms, draw knives and, like cats, begin to circle one another. Escamillo trips on a small rock, his knife blade snaps, and José is about to strike when Carmen, who has heard the quarrel, rushes in and grabs hold of his arm. The other smugglers quickly follow and separate the two men.

Escamillo, who has been trained to face death with grace, gathers himself up with dignity, remarks that he is "ravished" to have been saved by Carmen, offers to give José a return match any time he wishes, and invites everyone to his next performance in Seville, where he promises to perform brilliantly. "Anyone who loves me," he adds, looking meaningfully at Carmen, "will be there."

At this José tries once again to attack him but is held back by Remendado and Dancairo, and the Toreador makes a dignified exit to a slow and quiet version of the "Toreador Song."

The smugglers now begin to resume their work when one of them finds Micaela hiding behind a rock nearby. Still frightened, she brings up enough courage to tell José that his mother longs to see him again and will forgive him his desertion if only he will come to see her. Carmen, joined by others, advises him to return, for this is obviously no life for him. But José stoutly refuses to leave Carmen now and changes his mind only when Micaela adds what she had hoped not to have to tell him—that his mother is dying. After a word of warning to Carmen, he begins to leave with Micaela when Escamillo's voice is heard in the distance jauntily singing the "Toreador Song." Carmen, fascinated, starts running toward the path, but José bars the way and hurls her to the ground. Then, with Micaela, he goes.

ACT IV

The Prelude begins, appropriately for an introduction to a bright holiday scene, with the marked rhythm of a Spanish dance in which one can all but hear the stamping of feet. But quickly it subsides into a quieter melody based on an Andalusian dance called the *polo*, characterized by syncopation. It repeatedly is interrupted with sinuous scales. After some repetitions, it quietly fades out.

Posters on the walls of an ancient amphitheater on a sunny square in Seville boast that a bullfight will be held within, this very afternoon. Girls and men peddling fans, oranges, programs, water, and cigarettes mix in among the soldiers and ordinary citizens waiting to watch the expected procession of performers and officials to enter the amphitheater. There is holiday bustle and noisy, markedly rhythmic Spanish music. There may be dances executed by the ballet company, usually to music from Bizet's *L'Arlésienne*. Finally the procession comes, marching in rough formation into the ampitheater and headed by the local constabulary. There follow, in groups, the *toreros*, the *chulos*, the *banderilleros*, and the *picadors*, each with its special function to perform before, during, and after the bullfight. Each is separately greeted with rhythmic shouts and comments from the crowd. Finally, enter the matador—the foremost *torero*—himself, who is cordially greeted by everyone to the refrain of the "Toreador Song." He stops to bow again and again as hundreds of *Vivas* assail him while the orchestra plays the familiar, vigorous opening of the Prelude to the opera. At last he is permitted to pay some attention to the girl he has brought in on his arm. It is, of course, Carmen, and she is dressed to the nines. In a brief, sentimental, and not very passionate duet they assert that they love each other very much, whereupon Escamillo leaves his tigress to face his bull.

Then the Alcalde (the mayor) of Seville, accompanied by his own entourage, makes his formal entry into the ring, and everyone follows. Only Frasquita and Mercédès remain briefly behind to warn Carmen that José is lurking in the crowd and she had better leave quickly. For all three girls know perfectly well what may be expected from a young Spanish lover who has been betrayed. Characteristically, Carmen wants to challenge her fate, not run from it.

"Yes," she says, "I see him. I'm not the kind to be afraid of *him*. I'll talk to him right here." And the other two, with misgivings, follow the crowd into the arena.

José is pale, wretchedly clothed, his shirt torn, but Carmen shows absolutely no pity or lingering affection. She comes to the point at once.

"I've been told you were around here. Also that you might want to kill me."

But José claims he has come only to plead with her, to beg her to forget the recent past, to come away with him. He offers to join her band once more; he offers his love and faith. To all his passionate proposals she is absolutely adamant, for she loves him no longer and will always be free.

Does she, then, love the Toreador? Yes, she cries, she loves Escamillo and only him.

The entire argument has been punctuated by the fate theme and by bursts of victorious music from the amphitheater, and at this point the crowd inside loudly sings the "Toreador Song," indicating that Escamillo has won another victory. Carmen tears a ring from her finger—one José had given her in the days of their love—and hurls it contemptuously away. Excited now by the sounds proclaiming the prowess of her new lover, she tries to enter the theater herself.

But José stands in her way. Driven to desperation by rejection and jealousy, he draws his knife, seizes hold of Carmen, and stabs her to death.

With the "Toreador Song" still on their lips, the spectators come crowding out to find José on his knees by the side of the young woman. The fate theme thunders out as he cries brokenly:

"You can arrest me. I killed her . . . Oh, Carmen! My Carmen! . . . My beloved Carmen!"

RECORDINGS*

Bumbry, Freni, Vickers, Paskalis, Frühbeck de Burgos, Paris Th. Nat'l Op. Orch. & Cho. (1875 Opéra-Comique version)
3-Angel S-3767; 4X3S-3767 (cassette tape)
Excerpts from above   Angel S-36829
Callas, Gedda, Massard, Guiot, Prêtre, Paris Op. Orch.
3-Angel S-3650X
Excerpts from above   Angel S-36312; 8XS-36312 (cartridge tape);
4XS-36312 (cassette tape)
De Los Angeles, Micheau, Gedda, Blanc, Beecham   3-Angel S-3613
Excerpts from above   Angel S-35818
Price, Freni, Corelli, Merrill, Karajan, Vienna Phil. Orch. & Cho.
3-RCA LSC-6199
Excerpts from above   RCA LSC-2843; R8S-1036 (cartridge tape);
RK-1036 (cassette tape)
Resnik, Del Monaco, Sutherland, Krause, Schippers   3-London 1368

* Taken from Schwann-1 Record & Tape Guide, February 1973, and from Schwann-2 Record & Tape Guide, Spring 1973.

Excerpts from above   London 25924; M69104 (cartridge tape);
                                    M31104 (cassette tape)
Horne, Molese, Lewis (selections)   London 21055; M94055
                                                    (cassette tape)
Ludwig, Schock, Prey, Stein, Berlin Deutsche Op. (sung in German)
     (selections)   Seraphim S-60119

Stevens, Peerce, Reiner   3-RCA LM-6102
Wolff, Opéra-Comique, Paris   3-Richmond 63006
Excerpts from above   Richmond 23043
Arkhipova, Maspennikova, Del Monaco, Incninan, Melik-Pasheyev,
     Bolshoi Th. (selections)   Everest 3213E

SOME DEFINITIONS

ADAGIO — A tempo direction meaning slow.

AGITATO — A tempo direction meaning agitated, hurried.

ALLA MAZURKA — To be played like the Polish dance, the Mazurka, three beats in a measure, with the accent on the second beat.

ANDANTE AMOROSO — To be played leisurely and lovingly.

ARIA — An important solo song in an opera, oratorio, or cantata, which serves for extended soliloquizing and lyrical expression, in contrast with recitative (q.v.).

BARITONE — The male voice which lies between tenor and bass, often combining the weight of the bass with the lyrical pliancy of the tenor.

BASS — The deepest of the male voices.

BASS BARITONE — A male voice with a baritone range and a bass quality (Don Giovanni).

BASSO BUFFO — A bass voice suitable for comedy (Leporello in *Don Giovanni*).

BASSO PROFONDO — A heavy male voice of unusually deep register.

CLAQUE — A group paid to applaud or hiss an opera.

COLORATURA SOPRANO — An extremely flexible high soprano able to perform vocal gymnastics, in the form of rapid, florid, ornamented music.

CONTRALTO — The lowest voice in a woman (abbr. alto).

DIVA — The leading lady in an opera, the prima donna.

DRAMATIC SOPRANO — A large soprano voice with dramatic power.

DRAMATIC TENOR — A large tenor voice with dramatic power.

DRAMMA GIOCOSO — A jolly or funny play.

FORTE — Loud.

GRAND OPERA — Technically, an opera with no spoken dialogue, on a serious or tragic subject. The libretto is entirely set to music. However, Beethoven's *Fidelio* is an exception to this rule, for though it contains spoken dialogue, it is classified as grand opera because of the dignity of subject matter and music.

IMPRESARIO — The manager of an opera company.

LEITMOTIF — Literally, leading motive; a musical idea characterizing a person or episode which recurs in the music whenever that person or episode is recalled.

LIBRETTO — Literally, little book; the literary text of music, especially important in opera since it conveys in words the drama, emotions, and personalities expressed in the music.

LYRIC SOPRANO — Light, delicate, high soprano voice.

LYRIC TENOR — Sweet, not very powerful male tenor.

MEZZO — Half.

MEZZO-SOPRANO — The woman's voice that lies halfway between soprano and contralto.

MEZZO-TENORE — The man's voice that lies halfway between tenor and baritone.

MUSIC-DRAMA — A term often applied to Wagner's operas, in which the music is based on text and dramatic action, avoiding set arias and recitatives.

OPERA BUFFA — Opera which is comic to the point of farce.

OPERA GIOCOSO — Opera which is comic as opposed to serious or tragic.

OPERA SERIA — Serious, as distinguished from comic opera.

PIANO — A direction to play softly.

PREMIERE — The first performance in a given place. World premiere is first performance anywhere.

PRIMA DONNA — Principal woman singer in opera.

RECITATIVE — Musical declamation, half-spoken, half-sung, which in an opera serves for narrative, dialogue, or dramatic expression.

RECITATIVO SECCO – "Dry recitative" has the minimum instrumental accompaniment to the voice singing the recitative.

RECITATIVO STROMENTATO – "Instrumental" recitative has a comparatively varied instrumental accompaniment.

SOPRANO – The highest woman's or boy's voice.

TENOR – The highest adult male voice.

INDEX

Academy of Music, N.Y.C., *Aïda* performed in, 93
Adagio, defined, 167
Agitato, defined, 167
Aïda (Verdi), 65–94; cast, 65; critics on, 79–80, 88–89, 91; famous singers who have sung in, 92–93, 94; first performance at La Scala of, 90–91; freedom as Verdi's theme in, 66–67; history and origin of, 80ff.; opening performance in Cairo of, 87–91; recordings of, 67, 93–94; story and music of, 67–80
Alexander II, Tsar, 97, 102, 119
Alla mazurka, defined, 167
Amneris, in *Aïda*, 65, 67, 68–69, 71–79 *passim*; singers who have sung in role of, 93
Amonasro, King of Ethiopia, in *Aïda*, 65, 69, 73, 74–75, 76, 77, 78
Andante amoroso, defined, 167
Anna (Donna Anna), in *Don Giovanni*, 4, 5–8, 9, 10, 12, 17, 28, 30, 32
Anton, Prince of Saxony, 25
Aria, defined, 167
Arias: in *Aïda*, 67, 68; in *Don*

Giovanni, 31–34; in *Fidelio*, 45, 46, 49, 55–61
Arlésienne, L' (Daudet), 131
Arlésienne Suite No. 1, L' (Bizet), 131, 146, 162
Arroyo, Martina, 93
Artaria (music publishing firm), and Beethoven, 52, 53
Axur, Re d' Ormus (Salieri), 24

Bach, Johann Christian, 79
Balakirev Mily, 98, 101, 102
Bald wird sein Blut verrinnen (Soon his blood will flow), aria from *Fidelio*, 46
Ballet, in Bizet's *Carmen*, 146
Ballo in maschera, Un (A Masked Ball, Verdi), 80–82, 91, 125
Bara, Theda, 148
Barber of Seville, The (Paisiello), 18
Barbieri, Fedora, 93
Baritone, defined, 167
Barlow, Harold, 29
Bass, defined, 167
Bass baritone, defined, 167
Bass buffo, defined, 167
Bass profondo, defined, 167

176   INDEX

87; portrait of, 63; *Requiem* by, 144; *Sicilian Vespers* by, 92; *Simon Boccanegra* by, 81–82; work habits of, 85–87, 90

Verdi, Peppina (wife), 83, 86, 90

Victor Emmanuel, King of Italy, 81, 82, 91

Vienna, 22 (*see also* Theater an der Wien, Vienna; Vienna Opera); Beethoven's *Fidelio* in, 40ff., 46ff.; Bizet's *Carmen* in, 144ff.

Vienna Opera (*see also* Vienna): Mozart's *Don Giovanni* in, 12, 17–20, 22, 26, 28–29

Vocal and Opera Themes (Barlow and Morgenstern), 29

Wagner, Richard: Bizet and, 141, 144–45, 168; his operas classi-fied as music-dramas, 168; *Lohengrin* by, 89, 92; and Mozart, 3; and Mussorgsky, 104, 121; and Verdi, 84, 89, 91, 92

Waldmann, Maria, in Verdi's *Aïda*, 92–93

Weber, Aloysia, Mozart and, 15–16

Weber, Constanze. See Mozart, Constanze (*née* Constanze Weber)

Wen ein holdes Weib errungen (*He who has won a noble wife*), aria from Beethoven's *Fidelio*, 45

Yradier, Sebastián, 134

Zerlina, in Mozart's *Don Giovanni*, 4, 8–9, 10, 12–13, 17, 22, 26, 31